The Mill on

George Eliot

Simplified by Michael West

Revised by D K Swan

Longman

1800 word vocabulary

Longman Group Limited
London

Associated companies, branches and representatives
throughout the world

First published 1934
New edition 1962
13 impressions
This edition first published 1978

ISBN 0 582 52545 4

Words outside Stage 5 of New Method Supplementary
Readers and not explained in the text are in a list
on p. 100.

We are grateful to the BBC for permission to use
copyright photographs from their production of
Mill On The Floss. We also thank the following
Artists: Jane Asher for pages 46, 59, 74–75,
88–89, 97 and cover; Sonia Dresdel for page 17;
Betty Hardy for pages 88–89; Barry Justice for
pages 88–89, 97; Peter Kriss for pages 46, 74–75;
Joseph O' Conor for pages 88–89.

Cover photographs by Picturepoint Ltd., and
BBC.

Illustrated map by Trevor Ridley.

Contents

NORTH
NORTH SEA
ST. OGG
THE RIPPLE
THE RIVER FLOSS
THE STONE BRIDGE
MR. STELLING'S HOUSE
THE HOUSE
DORLCOTE MILL
THE RED DEEPS

Chapter 1
Dorlcote Mill

A wide plain—where the broadening River Floss hurries between its green banks to the sea. At the mouth of the river lies the little town of St Ogg. Ships come here loaded with wood or oil-seed or coal, and their red-brown sails are seen uplifted among the trees.

Just by the red-roofed town, a little stream, named the Ripple, flows into the Floss. How lovely the little river is with the dark, ever-changing colours of its water.

See those large trees whose branches overhang the stream...

Here is the stone bridge...

And this is Dorlcote Mill.

Even on this cold evening of leafless February the mill is pleasant to look at. The comfortable house of the miller is as old as the trees that shelter it from the northern winds, and the rush of the water under the mill-wheel is like a great curtain of sound shutting one off from the world beyond.

A little girl is standing near the edge of the water, and a white dog with one brown ear is jumping up and down at her side. She is watching the never-resting mill-wheel scattering its diamond shower of water as the stream turns it to grind the corn.

It is time she went into the house, for there is a bright fire to welcome her; its red light shines out through the window under the deepening grey of the sky. And her mother and father, Mr and Mrs Tulliver, are sitting there by the fire and talking.

'What I want,' says Mr Tulliver, 'what I want is...'

Chapter 2
Mr Tulliver decides about Tom

A good education

'What I want,' said Mr Tulliver, 'what I want is to give Tom a good education, an education that will help him to earn a living. That school where he is now would have been good enough if I meant to make a miller or a farmer of him; but I should like Tom to be a gentleman. I want him to be able to talk and write well; it would be a help to me when I bring cases in the law-courts. I don't want to make an actual lawyer of the boy, because I don't want him to be a rascal. I'd like him to be a business man or a land-valuer—like Riley. Riley looks Lawyer Wakem in the face as hard as one cat looks at another; *he's* not frightened of Wakem.'

'Well, you know best,' said Mrs Tulliver. 'I don't mind. But hadn't I better kill two nice fat birds and invite the aunts and uncles to dinner? Then you may hear what my sisters, Mrs Glegg and Mrs Pullet, have got to say about it.'

'You may kill every hen in the yard, if you like, Bessy; but I shall not ask the advice of any aunt or uncle about what I'm to do with my own son,' said Mr Tulliver.

Mrs Tulliver exclaimed, 'How can you talk like that, Mr Tulliver!—But you always do speak disrespectfully of my family. I say that it's lucky for my children to have rich aunts and uncles. However, if Tom is to go to a new school, I should like him to go somewhere where I can wash and mend his clothes. And, when the box of clothes is going to and fro, I might send him a cake or some apples. He will be glad to have the extra bit of food, whether they feed him well or not. My children can eat more than most children can—thank God.'

'Well, well,' said Mr Tulliver, 'we won't send him too far away for that. But what I'm thinking about is how to find the right sort of school to send Tom to . . .'

Mr Tulliver paused, and pushed both his hands into his

pockets as if he hoped to find some suggestion there. At last he said: 'I know what I'll do; I'll talk to Riley about it. He's coming tomorrow to settle that quarrel about the bridge. He's been educated himself. I want Tom to be a man like Riley, a man who can talk well, and has a good knowledge of business too.'

He paused again.

'What I'm afraid of,' he continued, 'is that Tom hasn't got the right sort of brains. He's a bit slow. He's like your family, Bessy.'

'Yes, he is,' said Mrs Tulliver; 'he takes a lot of salt on his food; my brother did that, and my father too.'

'Our little girl, Maggie, is more like my side of the family: she's twice as quick as Tom. Too clever for a woman, I'm afraid,' said Mr Tulliver, nodding his head seriously. 'An over-clever woman is like a long-tailed sheep—it doesn't add to her value.'

'All her cleverness makes her naughty,' said Mrs Tulliver, rising and going to the window. 'I can't keep her in a clean dress for two hours. I don't know where she is now, and it's nearly tea-time. Ah, I thought so!—wandering up and down by the water like a wild thing: she'll fall in one day and be drowned.'

Nine years old

Mrs Tulliver opened the window and called to Maggie to come in.

'You talk of cleverness, Mr Tulliver,' she said as she sat down, 'but I'm sure the child is half a fool in some things. If I send her upstairs to fetch anything, she forgets what she's gone for; and sometimes she sits on the floor in the sunshine and sings to herself like a mad creature while I'm waiting for her downstairs. That's not in my side of the family—nor is her brown skin either.'

'Nonsense!' said Mr Tulliver. 'She's as fine a girl as anyone could wish to see; and she can read as well as the priest.'

'But her hair won't curl—whatever I do to it.'

'Cut it off! Cut it off short,' said Mr Tulliver.

'How can you talk like that! She's nine years old, too big to have short hair. And her cousin Lucy has got a row of curls round her head. It seems hard that my sister Deane should have that pretty child.—Maggie, Maggie,' continued the mother as this small mistake of nature entered the room, 'what's the use of my telling you to keep away from the water? You'll fall in and get drowned one day! Don't throw your hat down there; take it upstairs. And change your shoes, and then go on with your needlework.'

'Oh, mother,' said Maggie in a cross voice, 'I don't want to do my needlework.'

'Not want to make a pretty tablecloth for your aunt Glegg?'

'I don't want to do anything for my aunt Glegg; I don't like her.'

Maggie went out, dragging her hat by the string, while Mr Tulliver laughed loudly.

'I'm surprised at your laughing at her, Mr Tulliver,' said the mother. 'You encourage her in her naughtiness; and her aunts blame me for not teaching her better.'

Chapter 3
Mr Riley gives advice about a school

A very important thing

'I've been thinking about something,' said Mr Tulliver as he turned his head and looked eagerly at Mr Riley.

'Ah?' said Mr Riley carefully. Mr Riley was a slow and solemn person; and for this reason Mr Tulliver had great faith in him.

'It's a very important thing,' he went on. 'It's about my boy, Tom.'

At the sound of this name Maggie, who was seated close by the fire with a book, looked up. Few sounds attracted Maggie's attention when she was reading; but Tom's name was like the loudest whistle. In an instant she was on the watch, ready to attack anyone who threatened danger to Tom.

'I want to send him to a new school—a really good school.'

'Well,' said Mr Riley, 'there's no greater advantage in life than a good education; although,' he added politely, 'a man can be an excellent miller or farmer without much help from the schoolmaster.'

'Ah, but I don't mean Tom to be a miller or a farmer. I shall give Tom a good education and put him into a business, so that he may make a nest for himself and not want to push me out of mine.'

Maggie was listening. Tom, she was sure, would never be wicked enough to want to turn her father out of his own home. She jumped from her chair and her book fell on the floor; then, running to her father, she said in a half-crying, half-angry voice:

'Father, Tom wouldn't be naughty to you—ever. I know he wouldn't.'

'What! No one must say anything against Tom, eh?' said Mr Tulliver, laughing. 'Well, he's a good boy.'

Maggie was satisfied and retired.

'It's a pity she wasn't the boy,' said Mr Tulliver when she had gone; 'she would have been clever enough to beat all the lawyers.'

'But your boy isn't dull, is he?' asked Mr Riley.

'Well, he is clever at things out-of-doors, and he's got a lot of common sense. But he's slow with his tongue; he hates books and spells badly—so they tell me; and you never hear him say clever things like the little girl. Now I want to send him to a school where they'll make him quick with his tongue and his pen, and make a clever fellow of him. I want my son to be equal to those people who have beaten me because they've had better schooling.'

'You're right, Tulliver,' said Mr Riley. 'Better spend money on your son's education than leave the money to him after you're dead.'

Mr Stelling

'Now I expect that you know of just the right school for Tom?' asked Mr Tulliver.

Mr Riley paused a long time before replying.

'I know of a very fine chance for anyone who has got the necessary money. The fact is, I wouldn't recommend any friend of mine to send a boy to a regular school, if he could afford to do better. A boy ought to get the best teaching, and he ought to be the companion of his master, and that master ought to be a very first-class fellow. And I know the right man.'

Mr Tulliver's face was eager. 'Well let's hear,' he said.

'He's an Oxford man, a clergyman. He's very fond of teaching, and wishes to keep up his studies. He's willing to take one or two boys as pupils. The boys would be treated as members of the family—always under Stelling's eye.'

'And how much money would Mr Stelling want?' said Mr Tulliver, who suspected that this wonderful man would demand a high price.

'Why, I know of a clergyman who asks a hundred and fifty pounds, and he's not as good as Stelling.'

'A hundred and fifty!' said Mr Tulliver. 'I never thought of paying so much as that.'

'A good education is cheap at any price; but Stelling isn't greedy. I've no doubt he'll take your boy at a hundred. I'll write to him about it if you like.'

Mr Riley was a man of business, and he knew his own interests. He knew very little about Mr Stelling—but Stelling was a son-in-law of Timpson, and Timpson was an important man in the place and could send Riley a lot of business.

And it is pleasant to be able to give advice when it is asked for.

Chapter 4
Tom is expected

It was a great disappointment to Maggie that she was not allowed to go with her father in the cart when he went to fetch Tom from the school; but Mrs Tulliver said that the morning was too wet. Maggie disagreed strongly. Soon afterwards Mrs Tulliver tried to brush Maggie's hair; but Maggie was revengefully determined that there should be no curls that day. Rushing from under her mother's hands, she put her head in a bowl of water.

'Maggie, Maggie!' exclaimed Mrs Tulliver, sitting helplessly with the brushes in her lap, 'what will be the end of you if you are so naughty? I'll tell your aunt Glegg and your aunt Pullet when they come next week, and they'll never love you any more. Oh, dear, oh, dear! Look at your clean dress, wet from top to bottom! People will think that...'

But Maggie could not hear the rest. She was on her way to a disused room at the top of the house—right under the roof—shaking the water from her head as she ran, like a dog escaped from his bath.

This room was Maggie's favourite hiding-place. She stayed in it, sobbing, until a sudden beam of sunshine came into the room. Then she ran to the window. The sun was really breaking through the clouds; the sound of the mill seemed cheerful again; and there was Yap, the white and brown dog, running about aimlessly as if he were in search of a companion.

She ran downstairs, looked along the passage for fear that she might meet her mother, then rushed out into the yard, where she danced round and round singing, 'Yap, Yap—

Tom's coming home!' And Yap danced round her.

'Hi! miss, if you dance round and round like that you'll fall down in the mud,' said Luke, the head miller, a tall, broad-shouldered man, black-eyed, black-haired, and covered with flour.

Maggie paused. 'Luke, may I go into the mill with you?' she asked. Maggie loved to wander round the great spaces of the mill: the continuous roar, the unresting movement of the great stones, the fine white powder over everything and the pure, sweet smell made Maggie feel that the mill was a little world apart from her everyday life.

She sat on a heap of corn near the place where Luke was working.

'If I lent you one of my books, Luke, would you read it?'

'No, miss. I'm not a reader. I've got to keep accounts of the corn and the flour, and I haven't time to know many things besides my work.'

'Why, you're like my brother, Tom. Tom's not fond of reading. I love Tom so dearly, Luke—better than anyone else in the world. When I grow up I shall keep his house and we shall always live together. I can tell him everything he doesn't know. I think Tom's clever, although he doesn't like books; he can make beautiful whips and rabbit-houses.'

'Ah,' said Luke, 'but he'll be very sad—because the rabbits are all dead.'

'Dead!' screamed Maggie, jumping up from her seat on the corn. 'Oh, dear, Luke! What, the one with big ears, and the spotted one that Tom spent all his money to buy?'

'All dead.'

'Oh, Luke,' said Maggie, while the big tears rolled down her cheeks, 'Tom told me to see that the man took care of them; he told me to go and see them every day—and I forgot! What *shall* I do? Oh, he'll be so angry with me; I know he will—and so sorry about his rabbits. And I'm so sorry too. Oh, what *shall* I do?'

Chapter 5
Tom comes home

Tom brings a present

Tom was to arrive early in the afternoon.

At last the sound of the wheels was heard. Mrs Tulliver came outside the door, and even held her hand on Maggie's uncurled head, forgetting all the griefs of the morning.

'There he is, my sweet boy!'

Mrs Tulliver stood with her arms open, and Maggie jumped first on one leg and then on the other, while Tom descended from the cart. He thought himself too much of a man to show any tender feelings. 'Hallo, Yap—are you there!' was his only greeting.

However, he let his mother kiss him; but, while Maggie hung on his neck, his blue-grey eyes wandered towards the river, where he intended to fish as early as possible tomorrow morning. He was just an ordinary boy—one of those boys that grow everywhere in England, and at twelve or thirteen years of age look all just alike.

'Maggie,' said Tom, taking her into a corner as soon as his mother had gone, 'you don't know what I've got in my pockets.' He nodded his head mysteriously.

'No,' said Maggie. 'How full they look, Tom! Is it nuts?'

'Nuts! No, silly; the nuts are still green. See here!' He drew something half out of his right-hand pocket.

'What is it?' said Maggie in a whisper. 'I can't see anything but a bit of yellow.'

'Why, it's a new. . .Guess, Maggie!'

'Oh, I can't guess, Tom,' said Maggie impatiently.

'Well, don't lose your temper, or I won't tell you,' said Tom, pushing his hand back in his pocket and looking determined.

'No, Tom,' begged Maggie, 'I'm not cross, Tom; it's only because I can't bear guessing. *Please* be good to me.'

Tom's hand slowly came out of his pocket, and he said, 'Well, then, it's a new fishing-line—two new ones—one for you, Maggie. I wouldn't buy any sweets at school just so as to save the money; and Gibson and Spouncer fought me because I wouldn't.—I say, we'll go and fish in the river tomorrow, won't we?'

Maggie's answer was to throw her arms round Tom's neck and hold her cheek against his without speaking—while he slowly pulled out some of the line. Then he said, after a pause, 'Wasn't I a good brother, now, to buy you a line all to yourself? You know I *needn't* have bought it, if I hadn't chosen to . . .'

'Yes, very—very good. . . I do love you, Tom!'

'Now I must go and see my rabbits.'

Tom is angry

Maggie's heart stood still with fear. She dared not tell the sad truth at once, but she walked after Tom in trembling silence, thinking how she could tell him the news in such a way as to soften his sorrow and make him less angry.

'Tom,' she said timidly when they were out of doors, 'how much money did you give for your rabbits?'

'Five and sixpence,' said Tom.

'I think I've got more than that in my box upstairs. I'll ask mother to give it you.'

'What for?' said Tom. 'I don't want your money, you silly thing. I've got far more money than you, because I'm a boy.'

'I want you to buy some more rabbits with it.'

'More rabbits? I don't want any more.'

'Oh, but, Tom—they're all dead.'

Tom stopped immediately in his walk and turned round towards Maggie. 'You forgot to look after them.' His cheeks became red for a moment, then pale again. 'I don't love you, Maggie. You shan't go fishing with me tomorrow. I told you to go and see the rabbits every day.'

He walked on again.

'Yes, but I forgot—and I couldn't help it, indeed I couldn't, Tom. I'm very sorry,' said Maggie, while the tears rushed fast.

'You're a naughty girl,' said Tom, 'and I'm sorry I bought you the fishing-line. I don't love you.'

'Oh, Tom, it's very cruel,' sobbed Maggie. 'I'd forgive *you* if you forgot anything. I wouldn't mind what you did—I'd always forgive you and love you.'

'Yes, you're a silly; but I never do forget things—I don't.'

'Oh, please forgive me, Tom; my heart will break,' said Maggie, shaking with sobs, holding on to Tom's arm and laying her wet cheek on his shoulder.

Tom shook her off, and stopped again, saying sharply, 'Now, Maggie, you must listen. Aren't I a good brother to you?'

'Ye-ye-yes,' wept Maggie.

'Didn't I save my money to buy you a fishing-line, and wouldn't buy sweets, and Spouncer fought me because I wouldn't?'

'Ye-ye-yes. . .and I. . .lo-lo-love you, Tom.'

'But you're a naughty girl. Last holidays you spoilt my paint-box, and the holidays before that you let the boat drag my fishing-line away when I'd told you to watch it, and. . .'

'But I didn't mean it,' said Maggie. 'I couldn't help it.'

'Yes, you could,' said Tom, 'if you'd attended to what you were doing. You're a naughty girl and you shan't go fishing with me tomorrow.'

With this terrible judgment Tom ran away from Maggie towards the mill, meaning to see Luke there and talk to him about the rabbits.

Maggie stood without moving—except for her sobs. Then she turned round and ran into the house, and up to her room under the roof. There she sat on the floor and laid her head against the wall, with a crushing sense of misery. Tom had come home, and she had thought how happy she would be—

and now he was cruel to her. What was the use of anything, if Tom didn't love her? Oh, he was very cruel! Hadn't she wanted to give him her money, and said how very sorry she was? She knew she was naughty to her mother, but she had never been naughty to Tom—had never *meant* to be naughty to him.

Maggie thought she must have been there for hours. It must be tea-time, and they were all having their tea and not thinking of her. Well, then, she would stay up there and eat nothing—hide behind that barrel, and stay there all night...

And then she heard a step on the stair.

Forgiven

Tom had been talking to Luke, walking round the garden, cutting sticks—too interested to think of Maggie and the effect his angry words had had on her.

Then he was called in to tea.

'Why, where's my little girl? Where's your little sister?' said his father and Mrs Tulliver almost at the same moment.

'I don't know,' said Tom.

'What! Hasn't she been playing with you all this time?' said her father. 'She's been thinking of nothing but your coming home.'

'I haven't seen her for two hours,' said Tom, beginning to eat a piece of cake.

'Goodness! she's got drowned!' exclaimed Mrs Tulliver, running to the window.

'No, she's not drowned,' said Mr Tulliver. 'You've been naughty to her, Tom, haven't you?'

'Perhaps she's up there under the roof,' said Mrs Tulliver, 'singing and talking to herself and forgetting all about meal-times.'

'You go and fetch her down, Tom,' said Mr Tulliver rather sharply, suspecting that the boy had been unkind to his little girl—or she would never have left his side. 'And be good to her, do you hear? Or I'll give you a lesson!'

It was Tom's step that Maggie heard on the stairs. She knew it was Tom's step. He stood still at the top of the stairs and said, 'Maggie, you're to come down.' But she rushed at him and threw her arms round his neck, sobbing: 'Oh, Tom, please forgive me—I can't bear it—I will always be good—always remember things. Do love me—please, dear Tom!'

She rubbed her cheek against his and kissed his ear in an aimless way; and there was a tenderness in the boy which made him forget his determination to punish her as much as she deserved. He actually began to kiss her, and say:

'Don't cry then, Magsie. Here, eat a bit of cake.'

She put out her mouth for the cake and bit a piece, and then Tom bit a piece, and they ate together.

'Come along, Magsie, and have tea,' said Tom at last.

Next morning they were sitting by the river-side, fishing.

'Look, look, Maggie,' said Tom in a loud whisper.

Maggie was afraid she had been doing something wrong as usual, but Tom drew out her line and brought up a great fish on to the grass.

Tom was excited. 'Oh, Magsie, you little dear! Empty the basket.'

Maggie did not know what she had done to earn this praise; but it was enough that Tom had called her 'Magsie' and was pleased with her. There was pure delight for her in the whispers and in the dreamy silences; she listened to the soft *plop!* of the rising fish and the gentle sound of the branches about her as if the trees and the grass and the water had their joyful whisperings too.

It was one of their happy mornings.

Chapter 6
The aunts and uncles are coming

Mrs Tulliver was busy making cakes; they were even lighter than usual; 'A breath of wind would make them blow about like feathers,' said Kezia, the maidservant, proud to serve under a mistress who could make such wonders. They were for the family gathering at which sister Glegg and sister Pullet were going to be asked about Tom's going to school.

Mrs Tulliver thought it would be wise to ask them. 'But I'd rather not invite sister Deane this time,' she said. 'She always tries to find fault with my children.'

'Oh, ask her to come,' said Mr Tulliver. 'I never get a talk with Deane now; we haven't seen him for six months. What does it matter what she says? We don't need her favour—or her money.'

'There's no one in *your* family who will leave any money to the children at her death; but there's my sister Glegg and sister Pullet saving money all the time.'

'Huh!' said Mr Tulliver. 'What do your sisters' bits of money matter, when they have so many to divide them among? Besides, your sister Deane might persuade them to leave all their money to her child.'

'Yes, sister Deane could easily persuade them, because my children are so troublesome with their aunts and uncles. Maggie is ten times naughtier when they come than she is on other days; and Tom doesn't like them—though that's natural in a boy. But Lucy Deane is such a good girl: you may set her on a chair and she'll sit there for a whole hour and never try to get off. I can't help loving that child as if she were my own.'

'Well, if you're so fond of the child, ask her father and mother to bring her; and ask if Lucy may stay a day or two. Won't you invite my sister, aunt and uncle Moss too?—and some of their children?'

'Oh, dear, Mr Tulliver, you know that my sisters and your

sister don't go well together.'

'Well, well, do as you like, Bessy,' said Mr Tulliver, taking up his hat and walking out to the mill.

Chapter 7
Enter the aunts and uncles

Mrs Glegg and Mrs Pullet

Mrs Tulliver had been a Miss Dodson. The Dodsons were certainly a good-looking family, and Mrs Glegg was not the least good-looking of the four sisters. It was the great day of the family gathering, and, as she sat in Mrs Tulliver's chair, one could see that, for a woman of fifty, she was very good-looking. (But Tom and Maggie considered her very ugly.) She was wearing her hat rather on one side—as she often did when she was on a visit and happened to be in a bad temper. She held a large gold watch in her hand and said to Mrs Tulliver, who had just returned from a visit to the kitchen, that it was half-past twelve.

'I don't know what is the matter with sister Pullet,' she continued. 'It was once the habit in our family for the sisters to arrive at the same time—and not for one sister to sit for half an hour before the others came. I am surprised at sister Deane; she used to be more like me.'

'Oh, they'll all be here in time,' said Mrs Tulliver. 'The dinner won't be ready till half-past one. But, if it's too long for you to wait, let me fetch you a piece of cake and a glass of wine.'

'Well, Bessy!' said Mrs Glegg with a bitter smile, 'you should know your own sister better. I never did eat between meals, and I'm not going to begin now.'

The sound of wheels was a very welcome interruption to Mrs Tulliver, who hastened out to receive sister Pullet.

Sister Pullet was in tears when her carriage stopped at Mrs

Tulliver's door. She sat still, shook her head sadly and looked through her tears at the distant sky.

'Why, what ever's the matter, sister?' said Mrs Tulliver.

Mrs Pullet slowly rose and got down from the carriage, followed by Mr Pullet, a small man with a high nose, small bright eyes and thin lips—he looked like a small fishing-boat beside a great sailing-ship.

'Well, sister, you're late; what's the matter?' said Mrs Glegg.

Mrs Pullet sat down carefully before she answered:

'Gone!'

'What is?' said Mrs Tulliver.

'Died the day before yesterday,' continued Mrs Pullet, 'and her legs were as thick as my body. Full of liquid, she was.'

'Well, she ought to be glad to be dead, whoever she may be,' said Mrs Glegg decidedly; 'but I can't think who you're talking of.'

'But *I* know,' said Mrs Pullet, sighing; 'it's old Mrs Sutton of Twentylands.'

'Well, she's no relation of yours, nor a close friend,' said Mrs Glegg, who wept only for relations—and only just so much as was proper for them.

Mrs Deane and Lucy

The conversation was cut short by the arrival of Mrs Deane with little Lucy; and Mrs Tulliver had to watch sadly while Lucy's beautiful fair curls were set in order. It was extraordinary that Mrs Deane, the thinnest and darkest of the Miss Dodsons, should have this child; and Maggie always looked twice as dark as usual when she was by the side of Lucy.

She did today when she and Tom came in from the garden with their father and Mr Glegg. Maggie had thrown off her hat very carelessly, and her hair was rough and without any curls. She rushed at once to Lucy, and Lucy put up the prettiest little mouth to be kissed; everything about her was pretty. Maggie looked so rough and dark and untidy beside her.

'Oh, Lucy,' she cried, 'you'll stay with Tom and me, won't you?'

Tom stood looking very uncomfortable, with a half smile on his face.

'Humph!' said aunt Glegg loudly, 'do little boys and girls come into a room without taking any notice of their uncles and aunts? We never did that when I was a little girl.'

'Go and speak to your uncles and aunts, my dears,' said Mrs Tulliver, looking anxious and ashamed. She wanted to whisper to Maggie a command to go and have her hair brushed.

'Well, how do you do. I hope you're good children,' said aunt Glegg in her loud voice. 'Look up, Tom; hold your head up.' Tom tried to draw his hand away. 'Put your hair behind your ears, Maggie, and keep your dress on your shoulder.'

'Well, my dears,' said aunt Pullet, 'I think you are growing very fast—too fast for their strength,' she added, looking over their heads at their mother. 'I think the girl has too much hair: you ought to have it thinned and cut shorter, sister; it isn't good for her health. That's what makes her skin so brown—don't you think so, sister Deane?'

'No, no,' said Mr Tulliver, 'the child's healthy enough; there's nothing the matter with her. There's red wheat as well as white, and some like the dark kind best. But I think that Bessie might have the child's hair cut short so that it would lie smooth.'

'Maggie,' said Mrs Tulliver, calling the child to her and whispering in her ear, 'go and get your hair brushed—do! I told you not to come in without going to Kezia first; you know I did.'

A terrible determination was forming itself in Maggie's mind.

'Tom, come with me,' she whispered, pulling his arm as she passed him; and Tom followed willingly enough.

'Come upstairs with me,' she whispered again, when they were outside the door. 'There's something I want to do before dinner.'

'There's no time to play at anything before dinner,' said

Tom, who was eager for the feast.

'Oh, yes, there's time for this. *Do* come, Tom.'

Snip! Snip!

Tom followed Maggie upstairs into her mother's room, and saw her go at once to a box. From it she took out a large pair of scissors.

'What are they for, Maggie?' said Tom.

Maggie answered by seizing the front of her hair and cutting it straight across above her eyes.

'Oh, my buttons! Maggie, you'll get into trouble for that!' exclaimed Tom. 'You had better not cut more off.'

Snip! The scissors cut again while Tom was speaking; and he began to think it was rather good fun: Maggie looked so queer.

'Here, Tom, cut behind for me,' said Maggie, excited by her own daring and anxious to finish the deed.

'You'll get punished, you know,' said Tom, nodding his head.

'Hurry up!' said Maggie excitedly.

The dark hair was thick and cutting it was fun. One delightful *snip!*—and then another, and another—and the hair from the back fell heavily on the floor.

Maggie stood with her hair cut off roughly and unevenly; but she felt a sense of clearness as if she had come out from a wood into an open plain.

'Oh, Maggie!' said Tom, jumping round her and laughing. 'Oh, my buttons! What a queer thing you look! Look at yourself in the glass! You look like the mad fellow we threw nuts to at school.'

Maggie felt a sudden fear; she had wanted to be free from her troublesome hair; and she had thought of the triumph she would have over her mother and her aunts. She didn't want her hair to look pretty—that was impossible; she only wanted people to think her a clever little girl and not to find fault with her hair. But now, when Tom began to laugh at her and say she looked like a mad person, the affair began to look quite different. She looked in the glass; and still Tom laughed and danced; and her cheeks began to grow pale.

'Oh, Maggie, you'll have to go down to dinner soon,' said Tom. 'Oh, my buttons!'

'Don't laugh at me, Tom,' said Maggie, as the angry tears began to fall.

'Now, now! don't lose your temper!' said Tom. 'What did you cut it off for, then? I shall go down: I can smell the dinner.'

He hurried downstairs and left poor Maggie with that bitter feeling of disaster, which was almost an everyday experience for her. It had been very foolish, and now she would hear more about her hair than ever...

'Miss Maggie, you're to come down at once,' said Kezia, entering the room. 'Lord! what have you been doing? I never saw such a sight!'

'Don't, Kezia!' said Maggie angrily. 'Go away! I don't want any dinner.'

'Well, I can't stay; I've got to bring it to the table....'

'Maggie, you little silly,' said Tom, looking into the room ten minutes later, 'why don't you come and have your dinner? There's lots of lovely things to eat, and mother says you're to come. What are you crying for, silly?'

Oh, it was terrible. Tom was so hard and he didn't care. If *he* had been crying on the floor, Maggie would have cried too. And there was that nice dinner; and she was so hungry.

But Tom was not entirely hard. He went and put his head near her, and said in a lower, comforting tone:

'Won't you come, then, Magsie? Or shall I bring you a bit when I've had mine?'

'Ye-e-es,' said Maggie.

'All right,' said Tom, going away. 'But you'd better come. There's the sweets and nuts, you know.'

Maggie's tears had stopped. Tom's kindness had made her feel better—and there were the sweets and the nuts.

'Father will stand up for you'

Slowly Maggie rose from amongst her scattered hair, and slowly she went downstairs. Then she stood at the door, looking in. She saw Tom and Lucy with an empty chair between them, and a plate of food in front of it. And she was very hungry. She slipped in and went towards the empty chair.

Mrs Tulliver gave a little scream as she saw her, and all eyes turned towards the same point as her own.

Maggie's cheeks and ears began to burn.

'Hey! what little girl is this?' said uncle Glegg, a kind-looking, white-haired old gentleman. 'Is it some little girl you picked up on the road, Kezia?'

'She's cut her hair herself,' said Mr Tulliver in a whisper to Mr Deane, laughing. 'Did you ever know such a child?'

'Why, little girl, you've made yourself look very funny,' said uncle Pullet—and perhaps in his life he never said anything so cruel.

'Disgraceful!' said aunt Glegg in her loudest, severest voice. 'Little girls who cut their own hair should be beaten and fed on bread and water—not come and sit down to dinner with their uncles and aunts.'

'Yes, yes,' said uncle Glegg, meaning to give a playful meaning to these hard words; 'she should be sent to prison, I think, and they'll cut the rest of her hair off there, and make it short all over.'

'She looks darker than ever,' said aunt Pullet in a pitying voice; 'it's very bad luck, sister, that the girl should be so brown. She'll find life difficult—being so brown.'

'She's a naughty child who'll break her mother's heart,' said Mrs Tulliver, with tears in her eyes.

All of them—all talking about her, talking against her!

At first Maggie was angry. Tom thought she was being brave and he whispered to her, 'Oh, my buttons, Maggie; I told you there would be trouble.' He meant to be friendly, but Maggie thought he was rejoicing in her shame. All her courage left her. She got up from her chair, ran to her father, hid her face on his shoulder and burst out into loud sobbing.

'Don't cry, my girl,' said her father, comforting her. 'Don't worry; you were right to cut it off if it troubled you. Stop crying, father will stand up for you: father will stand up and protect you.'

Precious words of tenderness! Maggie never forgot any of these moments when her father 'stood up for her'; she kept them in her heart, and thought of them long years after, when everyone said that her father had done very badly for his children.

Chapter 8
Mr Tulliver shows his strength of mind

After dinner Mrs Tulliver sent the children out into the garden.

Then, 'Mr Tulliver,' she said to her husband, who was busy talking to Mr Deane, 'it's time to tell the children's aunts and uncles what you're thinking of doing with Tom, isn't it?'

'All right,' said Mr Tulliver rather sharply. 'I don't mind telling everybody what I mean to do: I have decided to send him to Mr Stelling, a clergyman at King's Norton, a very clever fellow who will teach him well.'

There were sounds of surprise.

'Why are you going to send him to a clergyman?' said Mr Pullet.

'You'll have to pay a lot for that, eh, Tulliver?' said Mr Deane.

'Why,' said Mr Tulliver, 'you see, I've decided not to put Tom in my business of miller; I'm going to put him into a profession. I'm going to give him an education so that he'll be able to deal with lawyers and that sort of person, and give me some advice from time to time.'

Mrs Glegg made a sound which was a mixture of pity and scorn.

'It would be better for some people,' she said, 'if they would leave the lawyers alone.'

'What'll it cost you?' asked Mr Glegg.

'A hundred pounds a year, that's all. But it will be money that will bring in money to the boy later.'

'Ah,' said Mr Glegg, 'you may be right. But we who've got no learning had better take care of our money—eh, Mr Pullet?' Mr Glegg rubbed his knees and smiled.

'Mr Glegg, I'm surprised at you!' said his wife. 'Making jokes when you see your own relations rushing to ruin!'

'If you mean *me* by that,' said Mr Tulliver rather angrily, 'you need not worry yourself about me. I can manage my own affairs without troubling other people.'

Mr Deane tried to change the subject of conversation. 'Somebody told me that Lawyer Wakem was going to send his son—that deformed boy—to a clergyman.'

'Well,' said Mr Tulliver, 'Wakem is a rascal, but he's a clever one. If you tell me who Wakem's baker is, I'll tell you where to buy your bread!'

'But Wakem's son has got a deformed back; so it's more natural to send him to a clergyman. And Wakem's son is not likely to follow any business,' said Mr Glegg.

'Mr Glegg,' said Mrs Glegg, 'you had far better be silent. Mr Tulliver doesn't want to know your opinion, nor mine either. There are people in the world who know better than everyone else.'

'Well, I should think you are one of them,' said Mr Tulliver, getting angry again.

'Oh, I say nothing,' said Mrs Glegg scornfully. 'My advice has never been asked, and I don't give it.'

'It's the first time you've said that,' replied Mr Tulliver. 'Advice is the only thing you're too willing to give.'

'I have been too willing to lend, if I haven't been too willing to give,' said Mrs Glegg. 'There are relations of mine that I am sorry I lent money to.'

'You've had five per cent interest on the money you lent me, though I am your relation.'

'Bessy, I'm sorry for you!' said Mrs Glegg.

'Oh, sister, don't let's have a quarrel,' said Mrs Pullet, beginning to cry. 'It's very bad among sisters.'

'It *is* bad,' said Mrs Glegg, 'when one sister invites another sister to her house on purpose to quarrel with her.'

Mr Tulliver burst out again, 'Who wants to quarrel with you? It's you who are always interfering with people. I should never want to quarrel with any woman if she knew her proper position.'

'My "proper position"! I should never have met you if one member of my family hadn't married into a lower position than she should have done.'

'My family is as good as yours,' said Mr Tulliver '—and better, because it hasn't got such a bad-tempered woman in it!'

'Well!' said Mrs Glegg, rising from her chair, 'I'm not going to stay a minute longer in this house.'

'Oh, dear! Oh, dear!' said Mr Glegg sadly as he followed his wife from the room.

'Mr Tulliver, how could you talk like that!' said Mrs Tulliver, with tears in her eyes.

'Let her go,' said Mr Tulliver, too angry to be affected by tears. 'Let her go, and the sooner the better.'

Chapter 9
Mr Tulliver shows his weaker side

Five hundred pounds

'If sister Glegg asked you to pay her money back to her, it

would be very difficult for you to find five hundred pounds now,' said Mrs Tulliver that evening.

Mrs Tulliver had a peculiar power of saying things which drove her husband in the opposite direction from that which she desired; and this speech of hers made Mr Tulliver believe that it would *not* be difficult for him to raise five hundred pounds, that Mrs Glegg might do as she liked about asking for her money—he would pay it without being asked—that he did not want to be in debt to his wife's sisters.

Ordinarily Mr Tulliver found the world very difficult, and he acted slowly and timidly; but when he was angry, he acted surprisingly quickly. He was on his horse soon after dinner next day on his way to see his sister, Mrs Moss, and her husband. He had decided to pay back Mrs Glegg her five hundred pounds. His brother-in-law, Moss, owed him three hundred pounds; if Moss could pay up that three hundred it would not be 'very difficult' to find the money to pay Mrs Glegg.

The fact is that Mr Tulliver was thought to be a much richer man than he really was. He had his own mill and quite a lot of land, but he owed two thousand pounds of debt on it. A man who is always going to law against his neighbours is not likely to pay off his debts. Nor can a man pay off his own debts if he is kind-hearted enough to lend money to his sister who has married a poor man and has eight babies.

'Don't worry'

Mrs Moss heard the sound of the horse's feet and was already at the door, with a weary smile on her face, and a baby in her arms.

'Brother, I'm glad to see you. How are you?'

'Oh—well enough,' answered the brother. 'Your husband isn't in the house, is he?'

'No, he's in the field over there. George,' she called to one of the children, 'run and tell your father that your uncle has come. Won't you get down off your horse, brother?'

'No, no; I must be going home again at once.'

'And how are Mrs Tulliver and the children?'

'Oh, they're well. Tom is going to a new school, and that will cost a lot. I shall need that money.'

'I wish you would let the children come and see their cousins. My children do want to see their cousin Maggie. I know she likes to come. She's a lovely child; and how quick she is!'

If Mrs Moss had been the cleverest woman in the world, instead of one of the simplest, she could have thought of nothing more likely to please her brother than this praise of Maggie. In spite of his determination, his eyes became softer.

'Yes, she's fonder of you than of her other aunts, I think. She's more like our family; there's not a bit of her mother's family in her.'

'I think my girl Lizzy is like her. Come here, Lizzy.'

'Yes, they're a bit alike,' he said, looking kindly at the little person in a rather dirty dress. 'You've got a lot of girls, Gritty.'

'Four,' said Mrs Moss with a sigh, 'and four boys; they've got a brother each.'

'Ah,' said Mr Tulliver, trying to make himself hard again, 'but they mustn't expect to depend on their brothers.'

'No,' said his sister, 'but I hope their brothers will love them. The more there are of them, the more they must love one another. And I hope your boy will always be good to his sister, though there are only two of them—like you and me, brother.'

Those words went straight to Mr Tulliver's heart; he could compare his relation to his own sister with Tom's relation to Maggie. Would his little girl ever be in need, and would Tom be hard on her?

'Here's father,' said Mrs Moss.

Mr Tulliver got down from his horse and went with Mr Moss into the garden.

'I can't do without my money any longer,' said Mr Tulliver.

'I've got to pay five hundred to Mrs Glegg, and Tom is going to cost me money. You must see if you can pay me back my three hundred pounds.'

'Well,' said Mr Moss, 'I owe rent. I'll have to sell everything I've got to pay you and my rent too.'

'You must do what you can. I can't go without my money any longer. You must get it as quick as you can.'

Mr Tulliver walked quickly out of the garden, and got on his horse.

Outside the gate he stopped.

'Poor little girl,' he said aloud, 'she'll have nobody but Tom when I'm gone.'

He turned his horse and rode slowly back.

Mrs Moss was still on the doorstep; she had been crying.

'Don't worry, Gritty,' said Mr Tulliver in a gentle voice. 'I'll manage to do without the money for a time—but you must be as clever and careful as you can.'

Mrs Moss's tears came again.

'It's all right!' said Mr Tulliver very gently. 'My little Maggie shall come and see you soon. You mustn't worry... I'll always be a good brother to you.'

Mr Tulliver searched even harder for someone who was willing to lend him five hundred pounds.

'It must not be a friend of Wakem, the lawyer,' he said. But a friend of Wakem was the only person he could find.

The River of Fate had caught Mr Tulliver in its current, like a helpless feather in his own mill-stream.

Chapter 10
Tom at Mr Stelling's

Mr Tulliver left Tom at Mr Stelling's house and drove home in a very satisfied state of mind. He considered that it was a lucky moment for him when he thought of asking Riley's advice about a teacher for Tom. Mr Stelling had seemed so intelligent; he had talked in such a quick, sensible way—answering every difficult, slow sentence of Mr Tulliver's with, 'I see, my good sir; I see—' or, 'Of course, of course; you want your son to be a man who will be a success in the world.' Besides, he had asked Mr Tulliver's advice about feeding the cow, and had told several good stories. Stelling was clearly a man who knew everything—who knew exactly what Tom must learn in order to be equal to those lawyers.

It is not fair to laugh at Mr Tulliver, for I have known more highly educated people get wrong ideas, and for no stronger reasons than his.

Tom's sufferings during his first three months under the care of Mr Stelling were rather severe.

At his school, life had not been difficult. He was good at games—especially at fighting. Mr Jacobs, the headmaster, did not gain Tom's respect, nor fill him with any large amount of learning. It was impossible for Tom to imagine that any schoolmaster would be something entirely different from Mr Jacobs, or any school very different from that.

Tom soon found that life at Mr Stelling's house was a difficult business. He had to learn Latin, and he had to learn to pronounce English in a new way. He was timid—and that made pronouncing more difficult, so that he hardly dared say a single word in reply to Mr or Mrs Stelling, and even dreaded to be asked at table whether he would have more. But it was impossible to despise Mr Stelling as he had despised Mr Jacobs.

Young Tulliver was Mr Stelling's first pupil; if he made a success of Tom, other pupils would follow: so he was determined to succeed.

Mr Stelling always said that 'teaching came naturally' to him. Perhaps it was for this reason that he set about it in the same blindly natural way (and with the same lack of imagination) as is found in the animal world. Birds build their nests, ants build their ant-hills in just the same way as they have always built them even when they are taken to a different country where the old kind is quite unsuitable. So Mr Stelling taught Latin to Tom, just because he himself had been taught Latin at school, and in just the same way as Latin had been taught to him.

He soon decided that Tom was a thoroughly dull boy, and suspected that he was not trying to work his hardest. Tom had never had any difficulty in learning about dogs or horses and out-of-door things (less, perhaps, than Mr Stelling), but he certainly had difficulty in learning Latin.

'You take no interest in what you are doing,' Mr Stelling would say—which was true.

He was severe with Tom about his lessons, for he considered that Tom was a boy who would not learn without some severity. He was not a bad-tempered or hard man—certainly not; he joked with Tom at table and corrected his way of speaking and his behaviour in the most playful manner; but Tom had not been used to jokes like Mr Stelling's, and for the first time in his life he had a painful feeling that everything he did or said was wrong.

As for play—Tom went for long walks with Mr Stelling; although Mr Stelling said that he would arrange for a drill-master next half-year. Mrs Stelling thought it would be good for the boy to 'make himself useful' in his spare time; so she set him to watch her little daughter, Laura, while the nurse was busy with the younger baby.

How Tom longed for someone to play with! In his secret heart he longed to have Maggie with him; he would forgive all her mistakes, all her forgetfulness—if only she were here.

Someone to play with!—always Mr Stelling—only Mr Stelling—Mr Stelling all day—all the time!

Chapter 11
Maggie visits Tom

'I'll help you'

Before this miserable half-year was ended, Maggie actually came to visit Tom. Mrs Stelling had invited her to come and stay with her brother; so, when Mr Tulliver drove over late in October, Maggie came too.

It was Mr Tulliver's first visit to see Tom—the boy must learn not to think too much about home.

'Well, my boy,' he said to Tom, 'you look very well! School is good for you.'

Mr Stelling left the room to tell his wife about their arrival.

'I don't think I am well, father,' said Tom. 'I wish you'd ask Mr Stelling not to make me learn Latin. It always makes me feel ill.'

'Nonsense,' said Mr Tulliver, 'you must learn what your master tells you; he knows what it is right for you to learn.'

'I'll help you now, Tom,' said Maggie, trying to comfort and encourage him. 'I've come to stay for a long time, if Mrs Stelling asks me. I brought my box and my dresses.'

'*You* help me, you silly little thing!' said Tom, delighted at the idea of proving to Maggie that she could *not* help him. 'You couldn't do one of *my* lessons. Girls never learn such things. They are too silly.'

Mrs Stelling in her invitation did not mention a longer time than a week for Maggie's stay, but Mr Stelling took Maggie on his knee and asked her where she got her dark eyes from, and said that she must stay for at least two weeks. Maggie thought Mr Stelling was a charming man, and Mr Tulliver was quite proud to leave his little daughter where she would have an opportunity of showing her cleverness to strangers.

'Come with me into the library, Maggie,' said Tom as their father drove away. 'Why do you shake your head now, you silly?' he continued, for her hair was now brushed smoothly behind her ears.

'Oh, I can't help it,' said Maggie impatiently; 'don't worry me, Tom.'

'Oh, what books!' she exclaimed as she saw the bookshelves in the library. 'I should like to have as many books as that!'

'Why, you couldn't read one of them,' said Tom in triumph; 'they are all Latin.'

'No, they're not,' said Maggie; 'I can read the back of this one—*History of the Decline and Fall of the Roman Empire.*'

'Well, what does it mean? *You* don't know,' said Tom.

'Oh, I could find out,' said Maggie scornfully.

'Why, how?'

'I should look inside and see what it was about.'

'You had better not do that, Miss Maggie,' said Tom, seeing her hand on the book. 'Mr Stelling lets nobody touch his books without permission, and I shall be punished if you take it out.'

'Oh, all right; let me see all *your* books then,' said Maggie, throwing her arms around Tom's neck and rubbing his cheek with her small round nose.

A happy two weeks

Tom, in the gladness of his heart at having dear old Maggie to quarrel with again, seized her round the waist and began to jump with her round the large library table. Away they jumped, faster and faster, till Maggie's hair flew from behind her ears. At last reaching Mr Stelling's small reading-table, they knocked it over with a loud *crash*. Tom stood in terror for some moments, dreading the appearance of Mr or Mrs Stelling.

'Oh, I say, Maggie,' he said at last, lifting the table up, 'we must keep quiet here, you know. If we break anything, Mrs Stelling will be angry and scold me.'

'Is she a cross woman?' asked Maggie.

'She certainly is!' said Tom.

'I think all women are crosser than men,' said Maggie. 'Aunt Glegg is a great deal crosser than uncle Glegg, and mother scolds me more than father does.'

'Well, *you* will be a woman one day,' said Tom.

'But I shall be a *clever* woman,' said Maggie.

'Oh, yes; and a nasty proud thing. Everybody will hate you.'

'Oh, you oughtn't to hate me, Tom: it will be very wicked of you if you do, because I'm your sister.'

'Yes, but if you're a nasty thing, I *shall* hate you.'

'Oh, but Tom, you won't! I shan't be. I shall be very good to you—and I shall be good to everybody. You won't hate me really, will you, Tom?'

'Oh, I don't know!—Now it's time for me to learn my lessons. Look what I've got to do,' he said, drawing Maggie towards him and showing her his work. 'See how much you can understand of that.'

Maggie found the Latin quite interesting; she delighted in new words, and quickly found that there was a list of the Latin words with their English meanings at the end.

'Oh, Tom, it is such a pretty book,' she said. 'I could learn Latin very soon; I don't think it's at all hard.'

'I know what you've been doing; you have been reading the English at the end. Any silly can do that.'

This visit to Tom was a very happy time for Maggie. She was allowed to be in the library with him when he did his lessons, and she learned a lot more about Latin.

Mr Stelling was amused by her talk, and they were very good friends. She told Tom she would like to go to school with Mr Stelling and learn just the same things as he did: she felt sure she would be able to do the work.

'I'm sure you couldn't do it,' said Tom. 'I'll just ask Mr Stelling if you could.'

'I'll ask him myself,' said Maggie.

'Mr Stelling,' she said that same evening, 'could I do Latin and all Tom's lessons if you were to teach me instead of him?'

'No, you couldn't,' said Tom indignantly; 'girls can't do those things, can they sir?'

'They can learn a little of everything, I suppose,' said Mr Stelling. 'They have a great deal of cleverness of a sort. They are quick, but they do not go deep into things.'

Tom was delighted with this judgment, and showed his triumph by nodding his head at Maggie behind Mr Stelling's chair.

Maggie had hardly ever been so humbled. She had been so proud to be called 'quick' all her little life—and now it appeared that this quickness was something to be ashamed of. It would have been better to be slow like Tom.

'Ha, ha! Miss Maggie!' said Tom, when they were alone, 'you see it's not such a fine thing to be "quick". You'll "never go far into anything," you know.'

And Maggie was so upset at the thought of this dreadful fate that she did not even reply.

When this small 'quick but not deep' person was fetched away in the cart by Luke, the library was once more lonely for Tom, and he felt her loss terribly. He had really been brighter and had got through his lessons better since she had been there. She had asked Mr Stelling so many questions about the Roman Empire that Tom had actually begun to understand that there once really were people who were lucky enough to know Latin without having to learn it at school.

Chapter 12
The Christmas holidays

It was a real Christmas, with snow and frost. Aunt and uncle Moss came with all their children to Christmas dinner.

Christmas was as good as it had ever been since Tom could remember—better, because there was plenty of snow, and fights with snowballs and sliding on the ice.

And yet this Christmas Day was not quite so happy as it had always been before. Christmas was cheery, but Mr Tulliver was not. He was angry; he had enemies; his voice grew louder and louder as he told the story of his wrongs over the dinner-table. Tom felt that the world was full of rascals, and that the business of grown-up life meant a great deal of quarrelling.

The 'enemy' was Pivart. Pivart had land farther up the stream and was making channels to lead the water from the stream to it. Mr Tulliver's only male audience at the Christmas dinner was Mr Moss—but Mr Tulliver did not talk to prove anything to anyone; he talked to give expression to his own feelings. The good dinner had made Mr Moss sleepy; but Mrs Moss, interested in everything that concerned her brother, put in a word from time to time.

'Pivart is a new name in this place, isn't it, brother?'

'New name? Yes! It certainly is!' said Mr Tulliver angrily. 'Dorlcote Mill has been in our family for over a hundred years, and nobody ever heard of a Pivart touching the river, till this fellow bought Bincomb's farm . . . I'll *Pivart* him!' added Mr Tulliver, raising his glass.

'You won't be forced to go to law with him, I hope, brother,' said Mrs Moss anxiously.

'I don't know what I shall be forced to do; but I know what I shall force him to do, if there's any justice in the land. I know who is encouraging him—it's Wakem! I know Wakem tells him he's safe from the law; but there are other lawyers than Wakem. It takes a big rascal to beat him; but there's a bigger rascal to be found. Wakem lost in that affair of Brumley's . . . It's no good people telling me that Pivart's water-channels won't stop my mill-wheel; I know they will; and I know as much about water as any man—eh, Moss?'

Mrs Moss looked across the table at her sister-in-law. 'I'm

sorry to see my brother so angry and worried about this water business,' she said.

'It's your brother's way, Mrs Moss,' answered Mrs Tulliver. She always spoke of her husband as 'your brother' to Mrs Moss when his behaviour was *not* being admired.

Mrs Moss looked anxious. 'I hope and pray he won't go to law. The right doesn't always win in the law-courts. This Mr Pivart is a rich man, and rich men usually get what they want.'

'I think sometimes,' said Mrs Tulliver, 'that I shall be driven mad by all this talk about law and water. It's nothing but "law" and "water" now from when we get up in the morning until we go to bed at night. But I never stop him; I only say, "Do what you like; but whatever you do, don't go to law."'

As we have seen, what Mrs Tulliver said to her husband always seemed to make him do just the opposite; and what did more even than his wife's words to increase Mr Tulliver's eagerness to go to law, was the sight of Mr Wakem himself every market day. It was Wakem who had made Mr Tulliver lose in that earlier quarrel with Dix; and then again in that affair about the bridge. And, as a last drop of bitterness, he had been forced to borrow that five hundred pounds from a friend of Wakem. He would teach Wakem a lesson this time!...

'Father,' said Tom, one evening near the end of the holidays, 'uncle Glegg says that Lawyer Wakem *is* going to send his son to Mr Stelling. You won't like me to go to school with Wakem's son, will you?'

'It doesn't matter,' said Mr Tulliver. 'Don't you learn anything bad off him—that's all. The boy is a poor, deformed creature, and he's more like his mother than his father in the face. But it's a sign Wakem thinks well of Mr Stelling, and Wakem knows what's good.'

Mr Tulliver was secretly rather proud that his son should have the same education as Wakem's son. But Tom did not feel comfortable about it. If young Wakem hadn't been deformed, he might have had the chance of as many good stand-up fights as he wished; but. . .it was a pity Philip Wakem was deformed.

Chapter 13
The new school-fellow

'Well, Tulliver. We're glad to see you again,' said Mr Stelling cheerfully. 'Take off your coat and come into the library till dinner. You'll find a bright fire there—and a new companion.'

Tom felt very uncomfortable as he took off his coat. He had seen Philip Wakem at St Ogg, and had always turned away his eyes from him as quickly as possible.

'Here is a new companion for you to shake hands with, Tulliver,' said Mr Stelling, as they entered the library, '—Philip Wakem. I shall leave you to get to know each other by yourselves. Perhaps you have already met each other—you are neighbours at home.'

Tom looked confused, while Philip rose and glanced at him timidly. Mr Stelling wisely turned away and closed the door behind him.

Philip was both too proud and too timid to walk towards Tom; he thought that Tom disliked looking at him, and his deformity was most visible when he walked. So they remained without shaking hands or even speaking. Tom went to the fire and warmed himself, turning to look at Philip from time to time. Philip had sat down and was drawing on a piece of paper, and as he drew he was thinking what he could say to Tom.

Tom began to look oftener and longer at Philip's face. It was really not an unpleasant face—very old-looking, Tom thought. He wondered how much older Philip Wakem was than himself. He looked very pale and weak; it was clear he would not be able to play any real games—but he seemed to be able to draw well; he drew one thing after another without any trouble. What was he drawing?

Tom was quite warm now. It was certainly better to have even this deformed fellow as a companion than no one. He suddenly walked across the room and looked at Philip's paper.

'Why, it's a donkey with baskets!—and a dog, and some hens in the corn!' he exclaimed, his tongue loosened by surprise and admiration. 'Oh, my buttons, I wish I could learn to draw like that!'

'Oh, you can do them without learning; I never learnt drawing.'

'Never learnt! When I make dogs and horses, the heads and legs won't come right.' Tom thought he must not be too humble with this fellow. 'But I suppose I could do them if I tried,' he said.

'Oh, yes, it's very easy.'

'But haven't you been taught anything? I thought you'd been to school a long time.'

'Yes,' said Philip, smiling. 'I've been taught Latin and Greek—and writing, and such things.'

'Oh, but—I say, you don't like Latin, do you?'

'It doesn't worry me.'

'You wait till you get to the irregular verbs.'

'Oh, I've done with all that; I don't learn that stuff any more,' said Philip.

'Then you won't have the same lessons as I shall,' said Tom with a sense of disappointment.

'No—but I expect I'll be able to help you. I shall be very glad to, if I can.'

Wakem's son did not seem to be such an unpleasant fellow as Tom had expected.

'I say,' said Tom some time later, 'do you love your father?'

'Yes,' said Philip, going red in the face. 'Don't you love yours?'

'Oh, yes—I only wanted to know,' said Tom, rather ashamed of himself.

'I can't think why anyone should learn Latin,' said Tom, hastily returning to the earlier subject of conversation. 'I don't suppose Sir John Crake knows Latin, and he rides a horse better than anyone in the neighbourhood.'

'He learnt Latin as a boy, of course,' said Philip, 'but perhaps he's forgotten it now.'

'Well, I can do that, then,' said Tom.

Philip laughed. 'I remember things. And there are some lessons I'm very fond of. I'm fond of Greek history. I should like to have been a Greek and to have fought the Persians.'

'Are there any stories about fighting in Greek history?'

'Oh, yes: there are very fine stories of that sort about the Greeks.'

'I say, will you tell me them?' said Tom, jumping on one leg and then on the other.

'Why, yes. I know lots of stories besides the Greek ones.'

Tom wished to make things more equal.

'And I could show you how to catch fish,' he said. 'You could fish, couldn't you? It's only standing and sitting still, you know,' he said.

'I hate fishing. I think people look like fools sitting and watching a fishing-line hour after hour.'

'Ah, but you wouldn't say they look fools when they catch a big one! No!' said Tom.

Wakem's son, it was clear, was unpleasant in some ways, and must be kept in check.

Chapter 14
Tom and Philip

Tom sometimes felt friendship and sometimes dislike for Philip. He could never quite forget that Philip was the son of a 'rascal', yet he liked Philip's company—usually; and, besides, Philip helped him with his Latin.

Life was a little less hard for Tom during this second half-year. Philip was so advanced in his studies and such a quick learner that Mr Stelling was more interested in him than in Tom; for he could show good results far more easily with Philip. Tom was allowed to get through his lessons more easily; and he had Philip to help him. So he went on contentedly enough, learning a little at his own speed.

There was a great improvement in his manners and in the way he stood and walked. This was partly due to Mr Poulter. Mr Poulter was an old soldier who had fought with Wellington in Spain. He was employed to drill Tom, and he enjoyed the lessons as much as Tom did. The drill-lessons were mixed with stories of Mr Poulter's battles—which were much more interesting to Tom than Philip's stories about Ulysses and the other Greek heroes, who might have been imaginary—Wellington was (then) actually alive. It appeared that the company of soldiers in which Mr Poulter had served had taken a most important part in winning all the battles in which it had fought, and Wellington himself had expressed the greatest admiration for 'that fine fellow, Poulter', and the doctor who attended Poulter when he was wounded had been astonished at the wonderful way in which his flesh healed.

'Mr Poulter, I wish you'd bring your sword and do the sword-exercises,' said Tom.

One afternoon the sword was brought.

'Has it ever cut a man's head off?' said Tom, handling it with respect.

'Head off? Ah! and it would have if he'd had three heads! A sword's the best thing when you come to close fighting.'

Mr Poulter became so excited that he drew out the sword suddenly and Tom leapt back quickly.

'Oh!' cried Tom, 'if you're going to do the sword-exercises, let me go and call Philip. He would like to see you too.'

'What, that deformed fellow! What's the use of his seeing them?'

'Oh, he knows a great deal about fighting,' said Tom, 'and

how they used to fight with bows and arrows and battle-axes.'

'Let him come then. I'll show him something different from his bows and arrows!' said Mr Poulter, giving a trial swing with the sword.

Tom ran in to Philip. He was in the sitting-room playing the piano and singing—lost in the magic of his music, and entirely happy.

'Come, Philip,' cried Tom, bursting in. 'Don't stay there roaring "la-la-la"; come and see old Poulter do his sword-exercises in the yard.'

The charm of the music was rudely broken—broken in the most foolish, senseless way, for Tom knew (if he had thought for one moment) that Philip hated even to hear about the drill-lessons.

Philip turned red. 'Get away, you great fool!' he said fiercely. 'Don't come shouting at me; you're not fit to speak to a cart-horse!'

That made Tom angry too. 'I'm fit to speak to something better than you. You know I won't hit you because you're no better than a girl. But I'm an honest man's son, and your father's a rascal—everybody says so!'

He rushed out of the room and shut the door noisily behind him.

Mrs Stelling descended from her room to discover the cause of the noise. She found Philip sitting on the floor and weeping bitterly.

'What's the matter, Wakem? Why all this noise?'

Philip looked up and hastily dried his eyes.

'It was Tulliver; he came in to ask me to go out with him. I'm not well! I've—got a pain.'

Tom returned to the yard where Mr Poulter was performing the sword-exercises for his warmest admirer—himself. He took no notice of Tom's return: 'Ready! Cut! Point! Guard! One—two—three!'

'Mr Poulter,' said Tom when the show was ended, 'I wish you would lend me your sword to keep—just for a little while.'

Chapter 15
Maggie's second visit

This last quarrel between the two boys lasted longer than usual. Tom had been rude and rough; he had touched Philip's tenderest point, had caused him as much pain as if he had intended to wound him. Tom saw no reason why they should not make peace after this quarrel as they had done after many others—merely by behaving as if nothing had happened. But after a time he saw that his attempts to be friendly had no result, and he decided never to ask Philip to do anything for him again—not Latin, nor pictures, nor stories, nor anything. And they remained just polite enough to each other to prevent Mr Stelling from noticing anything.

Then Maggie came.

She could not help looking at Tom's new school-fellow with interest. She arrived in the middle of school-time and was present while Philip did his lessons with Mr Stelling. Tom had said in his letters, 'Philip knows lots of stories—not silly stories like yours'; from this, and from watching him do his lessons, she was sure that he must be very clever. She hoped he would think her clever too when she talked to him. And she had rather a tenderness for deformed things; she preferred lambs with bent necks, because the lambs which were quite strong and well made didn't care about being stroked and loved. She often wished Tom cared more about her loving him.

'I think Philip Wakem seems a nice boy, Tom,' she said when they went out of the library into the garden.

'Oh, he's a queer fellow,' said Tom shortly, 'and he's very angry with me because I told him that his father was a rascal. But you stop here by yourself for a few minutes, Maggie, will you? I've got something I want to do upstairs.'

'Can't I go too?' said Maggie, who, on this first day of meeting again, loved Tom's shadow.

'No; it's something I'll tell you about later—not yet,' said Tom, slipping away.

In the afternoon the boys were at their books in the library. Tom was reading his Latin book, moving his lips as if he were saying prayers; and Philip, at the other end of the room, seemed so interested in a big book that Maggie was filled with curiosity. Philip, looking up from his book, caught a pair of questioning dark eyes fixed upon him. He thought that Tulliver's sister seemed a nice little thing, quite unlike her brother; he wished *he* had a sister.

'I say, Maggie,' said Tom at last, shutting his books and putting them away hastily, 'I've done my lessons now. Come upstairs with me.'

'What is it?' said Maggie when they were outside the door. She remembered Tom's earlier visit upstairs and was suspicious. 'It isn't a trick you're going to play on me, is it?'

'No, no, Maggie,' said Tom in his sweetest voice; 'it's something you'll like ever so much.'

He put his arm round her neck and she put hers round his waist, and they went upstairs together.

'I say, Maggie, you mustn't tell anyone, you know—or I shall get punished.'

'Is it alive?' said Maggie, thinking that Tom might be keeping rabbits secretly.

'Oh, I shan't tell you,' said he. 'Now you go into that corner and shut your eyes while I get it ready. I'll tell you when to look. You mustn't scream, you know.'

'Oh, but if you frighten me, I shall,' said Maggie.

'You won't be frightened. Now shut your eyes—and don't look.'

Tom used a burnt stick to give himself large black eyebrows and a beard. He tied a red handkerchief round his head and another across his breast. Then he took the sword and held it with its point resting on the ground.

'Now look, Magsie!'

Maggie looked astonished for a moment, and Tom greatly enjoyed her look of wonder. Then she laughed and said: 'Oh,

Tom, you've made yourself look like Bluebeard in the theatre.'

It was clear to Tom that Maggie was not taking the sword seriously enough. He raised the sword and pointed it at her.

'Oh, Tom, please don't!' she said, moving backwards, away from it. 'I shall scream—I know I shall. Oh, don't! I wish I'd never come upstairs!'

'I'm Wellington! Quick march!' he said, stepping forward with the sword still pointing at Maggie. Her eyes were filled with tears and she got up on the bed as the only way of widening the space between them.

'Cut! Point! Guard! One...' Tom began to show the sword-exercises; using all his strength.

'Tom, I will not bear it. I *will* scream,' said Maggie. 'You'll hurt yourself; you'll cut your head off!'

'—two—three,' said Tom. At 'two' his arm trembled a little. 'Three' came more slowly, and with it the sword swung downwards. And Maggie gave a loud cry. The sword had fallen with its edge on Tom's foot; and, one moment later, he had fallen too.

She leapt off the bed still screaming.

There was a rush of footsteps towards the room.

Mr Stelling found her shaking Tom madly; she thought he was dead, poor child, and yet she shook him as if that would bring him back to life.

In another minute she was sobbing with joy because Tom had opened his eyes... She could not be sorry that he had wounded his foot; it seemed as if all happiness depended on his being alive.

Chapter 16
The end of a quarrel

Tom bore his severe pain like a hero; but there was a terrible fear in his mind—a thought so fearful that he dared not even ask the question which might bring the dreaded answer 'Yes.'

He dared not ask the doctor or Mr Stelling, 'Will my foot be deformed?'

He controlled himself so as not to cry out at the pain when the wound was washed each day, but when he was left alone, with Maggie by his bedside, the children sobbed together with their heads on the same pillow. Tom was thinking of himself dragging a deformed foot after him as he walked; and Maggie, who did not guess what was in his mind, wept to keep him company.

Neither Mr Stelling nor the doctor guessed that this fear was in Tom's mind. But Philip watched the doctor go out of the house, then went to Mr Stelling and asked that question which Tom had not dared to ask for himself.

'Excuse me, sir; does the doctor say that Tulliver's foot will heal perfectly, or will it be—be deformed?'

'Oh, no, oh, no. It will be perfectly all right, though of course it will take time to heal.'

'Did he tell Tulliver that?'

'No; nothing was said on that subject.'

'Then may I go and tell him, sir?'

'Yes, of course. I suppose he may be worrying about that. Go to his bedroom, but be very quiet...'

Philip stepped timidly up to Tom's bed.

'The doctor says that you will soon be all right again, Tulliver. Did you know that? I've just asked Mr Stelling, and he says that you'll walk as well as ever when your foot is healed.'

Tom felt that sudden stopping of the breath which comes with unhoped-for joy. Then he gave a long sigh, and turned his blue eyes on Philip's face, as he had not done for ten days or more. As for Maggie—she had not thought of this possibility; even the idea of it made her weep again.

'Don't be silly, Magsie,' said Tom tenderly, feeling very brave now, 'I shall soon be well.'

'Goodbye, Tulliver,' said Philip, putting out his small, delicate hand, which Tom took in his own strong fingers.

'I say,' said Tom, 'ask Mr Stelling to let you come and sit with me sometimes, Wakem—and tell me those Greek stories.'

Chapter 17
Philip and Maggie

Philip now spent all his time, out of school hours, with Tom and Maggie. Tom listened with great interest to a new story of Philip's about a man called Philoctetes, who had a very bad wound in his foot and cried out so much that his companions put him on an island with nothing but some poisoned arrows to kill animals for his food.

'*I* didn't roar a bit,' said Tom, 'and I'm sure my foot was as bad as his. Only cowards roar when they're hurt.'

Maggie asked whether Philoctetes had a sister and why she didn't go with him on the island.

One day, soon after Philip had told this story, he and Maggie were in the library together. Philip was at his books. Maggie wandered round the room, then went and leaned on the table near Philip to see what he was doing—they felt quite old friends now.

'What are you reading about in Greek?' she said.

'About Philoctetes,' he answered, looking up at her.

'Maggie,' said Philip after a moment, 'if you had a brother like me, do you think you would have loved him as much as Tom?'

Maggie's thoughts had wandered. 'Eh?—oh, better,' she said. 'No, not better than Tom. But I should be so sorry—*so* sorry for you.'

Philip went red in the face, and his eyes showed how much she had wounded him. Maggie felt that she had said the wrong thing.

'But you're so clever, Philip, and you can play music and sing,' she added quickly. 'I wish you were my brother.'

'But you'll go away soon, and you'll forget all about me. And when I see you after you've grown up, you'll hardly take any notice of me.'

'Oh, no; I shall not forget you, I'm sure,' said Maggie. 'I never forget anything. I think about everybody when I'm away from them. I think about poor Yap—he's got a bad throat and Luke says he'll die—but don't tell Tom that. You never saw Yap: he's a queer little dog.'

'Do you care as much about me as you do about Yap?' said Philip, smiling sadly.

'Oh, yes, of course!' said Maggie, laughing.

'I am very fond of you, Maggie; I shall never forget *you*,' said Philip. 'When I'm very unhappy I shall always think of you and wish I had a sister with dark eyes just like yours.'

'Why, I think you're fonder of me than Tom is,' said Maggie rather sorrowfully. She put her arm round his neck and kissed him. 'There now,' she said, 'I shall always remember you; and I'll kiss you when I see you again, even if it's a very long time.'

Mr Tulliver came a few days later to fetch Maggie.

'Oh, father,' said Maggie, 'Philip Wakem is so very good to Tom, and he's so clever. I do love him—and you love him too, Tom, don't you?'

Tom seemed rather confused. He looked at his father. 'I shan't be friends with him after I leave school; but we've ended our quarrel now, since my foot has been bad. He's taught me to play chess, and I sometimes beat him.'

'Well, well,' said Mr Tulliver, 'if he's good to you, pay it back to him and be good to him. He's a poor, deformed creature and looks like his dead mother. But don't be too friendly with him; he's got his father's blood in him too. And bad blood shows itself—in man, as in horses. Never trust bad blood!'

Chapter 18
The end of childhood

Maggie was thirteen years of age and was growing fast. She was at Miss Firniss's School, with her cousin Lucy. In her early letters to Tom she always 'sent her love' to Philip, and she asked many questions about him—which Tom usually did not answer. She was sad to hear Tom say in the holidays that Philip was 'still queer', and she could see that they were no longer friends. She did not see Philip again for a very long time, because he was always away in the summer. When they did meet, she was quite a 'young lady', and she—shook hands with him.

Mr Tulliver went to law against Mr Pivart; and Wakem was Pivart's lawyer. Maggie noticed that even the sound of Wakem's name made her father angry. 'Have as little as possible to do with young Wakem at school,' he said to Tom. Tom did not find this difficult, since Stelling had now two more pupils.

Tom had reached his last half-year at Stelling's school. He was a tall youth now. He stood up straight; he walked in a manly way, and when he spoke it was with a curious mixture of timidity and pride, which was rather pleasing.

Philip had left the school and had gone to the south of France for the sake of his health. This had helped to give Tom that unsettled feeling which is usual in the last few months of school. There was, too, some hope that his father's affair would soon be decided in the law-court; and that made the thought of going home more pleasant to Tom. For Tom, who had heard only his father's account of the matter, had no doubt that Pivart would be beaten.

It was nine o'clock on a cold morning towards the end of November, and Tom was sitting in the library, when Mrs Stelling entered to tell him that his sister was in the sitting-room.

Maggie was tall now; she was almost as tall as Tom, and she really looked older than he did at that moment. She had taken off her hat, and her young face had a strangely worn and tired look, as her eyes turned anxiously towards the door.

When Tom entered she did not speak, but only went up to him, put her arms round his neck and kissed him.

'Why have you come so early this cold morning, Maggie? And why aren't you at school? The holidays haven't begun yet.'

'Father wanted me at home,' said Maggie, with a slight trembling of her lips. 'I came home three or four days ago.'

'Isn't my father well?' said Tom rather anxiously.

'Not quite,' said Maggie. 'He's very unhappy, Tom. That affair—Pivart—I came to tell you; it would be better for you to know before you come home...'

'My father hasn't lost?' Tom sprang up from his chair and stood in front of Maggie, his hands deep in his pockets.

'Yes, dear Tom,' said Maggie, looking up at him.

Tom stood silent for a minute or two, with his eyes fixed on the floor.

'My father will have to pay a good deal of money, then?'

'Yes,' said Maggie rather faintly. '...Oh, Tom, he will lose the mill and the land and everything; he will have nothing left.'

Tom's eyes flashed one look of surprise at her; then he turned pale and trembled. He said nothing, but sat down again and gazed sightlessly out of the window. Tom had never been anxious about the future; he had always thought of his father as a man who was fairly rich; he had never dreamed that he would be unable to pay his debts— 'respectable' people don't behave like that, and he had a strong sense of the respectability of his family.

Tom's voice had the deeper note of manhood, but his thoughts were still boyish dreams.

Maggie was frightened at Tom's pale, trembling silence. She

threw her arms round him at last. 'Oh, dear, dear Tom, don't grieve so much; try to bear it well.'

Tom turned towards her, and tears gathered in his eyes. He rubbed them away with his hand.

'I shall go home with you, Maggie,' he said. 'Didn't my father say I was to go?'

'No, Tom,' she answered, 'father didn't say so.' What would he do when she had told him all? 'But mother wants you to come. Poor mother!—she cries so. Oh, Tom, it's very bad at home.'

Maggie's lips grew whiter, and she began to tremble almost as Tom had done. When she spoke again, it was like a faint whisper: 'And...and...poor father...'

She could not say it.

The thought of prison entered Tom's mind. 'Where is my father?' he said impatiently. 'Tell me, Maggie.'

'He's at home,' said Maggie. 'But,' she added after a pause, 'he's—not himself...He fell off his horse...He has known nobody but me ever since...He seems to have lost his senses. ...Oh, father, father...'

Tom tightened his arm round Maggie. His face was white and tearless, and his eyes saw nothing.

'We must go, Tom,' said Maggie at last; 'father will miss me.'

Tom rose.

'Wait a minute; I must speak to Mr Stelling and then we'll go.'

Chapter 19
What had happened

When Mr Tulliver first learnt that the judgment had gone against him, and that Pivart and Wakem had triumphed, everyone thought he bore the shock very well. He thought so himself; he thought that, if Wakem and Pivart imagined he was crushed, he would show them that they were very much mistaken. Of course he saw that the costs of the affair would take more money than he possessed. But there was Furley, who had lent him money on part of his land: he had an agreement with Furley that, if the money was not paid back within twenty years, Furley might take the land. Furley would certainly be glad to buy the whole estate including the mill, and would certainly keep Mr Tulliver at a very small wage to manage it for him. Furley was a business man and would see that this would be a very profitable opportunity for him. Mr Tulliver talked to Mr Gore, his lawyer, about this after they came out of the law-court, and asked him to see Mr Furley at once. Mr Gore promised to see Furley the next morning.

Then Mr Tulliver mounted his horse to ride home.

As he passed the post office he stopped. He longed to have Maggie near him—he did not know why. He sent a letter to Miss Firniss's school which would be delivered in the morning; she must come back at once—tomorrow. His hand trembled as he wrote.

Mrs Tulliver burst into tears when he told her the news; he was angry with her and told her that there was nothing to grieve about, and that he would have no difficulty in meeting the cost.

Next day Mr Tulliver was again on horseback in the afternoon, on his way to Mr Gore's office at St Ogg. Mr Gore ought to have seen Furley in the morning. But Mr Tulliver had not gone half-way when he met a clerk from Mr Gore's office, who said, 'Mr Gore has been called away from his office by an important affair, and he was unable to wait and see you. He will be able to see you at eleven tomorrow morning. Meanwhile he has sent you some important information in this note.'

'Oh,' said Mr Tulliver, taking the letter but not opening it, 'tell Mr Gore that I'll see him tomorrow'; and he turned his horse.

The clerk noticed Mr Tulliver's excited glance, and looked after him for a few moments; then rode away. Mr Tulliver put the letter in his pocket, thinking he would open it at home—reading was not an easy task to him. Later he thought that there might be something in the letter which Mrs Tulliver must not know, and it would be better for her not to see it.

He stopped his horse, took out the letter and read it. It was only a short note:

I have learnt from a secret, but trustworthy, source that Furley has lately been in great need of money; he has been raising money on all his property and has sold his rights in the Tulliver property to—Wakem.

Half an hour later Mr Tulliver's own cart man found him lying by the roadside, unconscious, with the open letter near him, and his grey horse standing by his side.

He was carried home, and Dr Turnbull was called.

Before Maggie reached home her father had already recovered consciousness. He had whispered something about a letter. Gore's letter was brought and laid on the bed. He lay for some time with his eyes fixed on it as if he was trying to join up his thoughts again with its help. Then a new wave of memory seemed to come, and swept the other away. He turned his eyes to the door as if trying to see something through the dimness of his eyes. 'My little girl,' he whispered.

'My little girl,' he repeated from time to time, unconscious of everything except this one all-important need—unconscious even of his wife. Mrs Tulliver ran backwards and forwards to the gate to see if Maggie was coming.

At last she arrived.

'Oh, mother, what's the matter?' she said with pale lips as her mother came towards her crying.

Dr Turnbull came to meet her.

Maggie ran towards the kind old friend whom she

remembered as long as she remembered anything; and he answered her trembling, questioning look.

'Don't alarm yourself too much, my dear,' he said, taking her hand. 'Your father has had a sudden attack of illness, and has not quite recovered his memory. But he has been asking for you, and it will be good for him to see you. Keep as quiet as you can.'

Her father's eyes were still turned towards the door when she entered, and she met in them that strange, longing, helpless look that had been watching for her arrival. With a sudden movement he raised himself in bed, and she ran to him and threw her arms round him in a passion of tears and kisses.

But that flash of recognition had been too much for him; he fell back stiff and unconscious on the bed again.

Mrs Tulliver wanted to have Tom fetched home. She sat crying at night: 'My poor boy, my poor boy; he ought to come home.'

'Let me go for him and tell him,' said Maggie. 'I'll go tomorrow morning—if father doesn't know me and want me.'

Next morning Maggie went.

As they came along the road, the brother and sister talked to each other in whispers.

'They say that Mr Wakem has bought the debt on the land, Tom, and can take possession of it,' said Maggie. 'It was the letter with that news in it that made father ill, I think.'

'I believe the rascal has been planning all the time to ruin my father,' said Tom. 'When I'm a man I'll make him sorry for it! You must never speak to Philip again.'

'Oh, Tom! I . . .'

But she was silent; there was no fight left in her.

Chapter 20
Mrs Tulliver's treasures

When Maggie reached home it was five hours since she had started out; and she was thinking with some trembling that her father had perhaps missed her and had asked for his 'little girl'.

She hurried along the path and was just opening the door when Tom came up, and they both looked into the sitting-room together. There was a rough-looking man sitting in her father's chair with a bottle and glass beside him.

The truth flashed on Tom's mind in an instant. He knew what this meant: the law-officers were in the house. The Tullivers were going to be 'sold up'. He had heard of such things; they were part of the disgrace and misery of losing all one's money and being ruined.

'How do you do, sir,' said the man, taking the pipe out of his mouth.

Tom turned away hastily without speaking: the sight was too hateful.

Maggie had not understood. 'Who is it, Tom?' she asked. 'What's the matter?'

Then she rushed upstairs and entered her father's room. Her father was lying with his eyes closed as he had been when she had left him. A servant was there, but not her mother.

'Where's my mother?' she whispered. The servant did not know. Maggie crept out of the room and said to Tom, 'Father's lying quiet. Let's go and look for mother. I wonder where she is.'

Mrs Tulliver was not downstairs—not in any of the bedrooms. There was only one more room; it was the store-room where her mother kept all her precious 'best things', that were only unwrapped and brought out on special occasions.

Tom opened the door of the store-room and immediately said, 'Mother!'

Mrs Tulliver was sitting among all her carefully stored

treasures. One of the chests was opened: the silver teapot was unwrapped from its many coverings of paper, the best china and the silver teaspoons were spread out on the table, and the woman was shaking her head over the mark *'Elizabeth Dodson'* on the corner of a tablecloth which she held in her hand.

She dropped it and stood up as Tom spoke. 'Oh, my boy, my boy,' she said, 'I never expected to see this day! We're ruined. . . . Everything's going to be sold up. We've got nothing. . . . We shall be beggars. Look at these tablecloths that I made myself and sewed the name on the corner; and they'll all be sold—and go into strange people's houses, and perhaps be cut with knives.'

'But will my aunts let the things be sold, mother? Do they know about it?' said Tom fiercely.

'Yes, I sent Luke at once. Your aunt Pullet has been here; but she cried and cried and said that your father had disgraced the family. And I did say to him again and again, "Whatever you do, don't go to law"—and what more could I do? I shouldn't have worried so much if we could have kept the things with my name on them. Your uncle Glegg has been too, and he says that things must be bought by the family for us to use, but that he must first talk to your aunt, and they're all coming to discuss the situation. But I know none of them will buy these cups because they all found fault with them when I bought them; they didn't like them. I bought them with my own money—your father never paid for them. Oh, why did he marry me and bring me to this?'

She burst out crying.

Maggie had listened to this speech with gathering anger. Why did they blame her father who was lying there upstairs in a sort of living death?

'Mother,' she cried, 'how can you talk like that?—as if you cared only for things. How can you care for anything but dear father himself—when he's lying there and may never speak to us again? Tom, you ought to say so too; you oughtn't to let anyone find fault with my father.'

Tom was a little shocked at Maggie's outburst—telling him and his mother what it was right to do! But after a time he went into his father's room; and his heart was filled with sorrow. He sat by the bed. Maggie went to him and put her arm round his neck, and the two children forgot everything else in the sense that they had one father and one sorrow.

Chapter 21
The family council

'We must all do the best we can'

It was eleven o'clock next morning when the aunts and uncles came.

Mr Deane was not coming—he was away on business, but Mrs Deane appeared in a fine new carriage with a smart servant driving it. She was the first to arrive.

'Oh, sister,' said Mrs Tulliver as she met her, 'what a world this is! What trouble!'

'Yes,' replied Mrs Deane; 'and we do not know today what may happen tomorrow. But we must suffer our troubles bravely.'

Mrs Deane made well-considered speeches on such occasions, and repeated them afterwards to her husband, asking him if she had not 'spoken very properly'.

Mr and Mrs Glegg came next, and were almost immediately followed by Mr and Mrs Pullet.

Mrs Pullet entered crying, as usual. Mrs Glegg was dressed in the deepest black as if for a funeral.

'Well,' said Mr Glegg, 'and how's the poor man upstairs?'

'Dr Turnbull thought that he was better this morning,' said Mrs Tulliver; 'he took more notice and spoke to me; but he hasn't recognised Tom yet. He looks at the poor boy as if he were a stranger; but he said something once about Tom and the little horse.'

'Well,' said Mr Glegg kindly, 'we must all do the best we can. When the things are sold we must all of us buy just what's enough for you, Mrs Tulliver—useful plain things—a table, a chair or two, and kitchen things, and a bed.'

'I do wish you would buy the silver teapot and the table-cloths with my name on them,' said Mrs Tulliver eagerly.

'Haven't Mr and Mrs Moss seen you?' asked uncle Pullet. 'Mr Tulliver has done a lot for them; and, if he has lent them money, they ought to be made to pay it back.'

'Oh, dear,' said Mrs Tulliver, 'I never told them, and they live so far away that they never hear anything except when Mr Moss goes to market. I wonder why Maggie didn't think of them; she was always so fond of her aunt Moss.'

Tom and Maggie speak out

'Why don't your children come in?' said Mrs Pullet at the mention of Maggie. 'They should hear what their aunts and uncles have got to say.'

Mrs Tulliver went upstairs to fetch Tom and Maggie, who were both in their father's room. On her way down again the sight of the store-room door suggested a thought to her, and she left the two children to go down by themselves.

The aunts and uncles appeared to have been in warm discussion when the brother and sister entered.

They shook hands in silence, till uncle Pullet said, as Tom approached him:

'Well, young sir, we've been talking about you. Your education ought to be useful now, I should think.'

'Yes,' said uncle Glegg, 'now's the time to show us what good your learning has been. Let's see whether you can do better than I can. I made my fortune without it. But I'm afraid that soft living and high learning will make it harder for you than it was for me.'

'Oh, he *must* do it,' said aunt Glegg, 'whether it's hard or not. He can't trust his friends to keep him; and Maggie must make up her mind to be humble and work, because there will be no servants to wait on her now.'

Tom was looking very far from humble, and he was preparing to say something—when his mother entered.

Poor Mrs Tulliver had in her hands the silver teapot.

'Look, sister,' she said to Mrs Deane as she set it on the table, 'I thought perhaps you'd like to look at it again, as it is a long time since you last saw it. I should hate for them to buy this at the hotel—my teapot that I had when I was married! Think of it being put in front of travellers, with my name on it. Look!—*Elizabeth Dodson*—it would be a disgrace to the family.'

'Disgrace!' said Mrs Glegg. 'The disgrace is to have married a man who has brought you to ruin.'

Maggie jumped up from her seat; no one should speak against her father.

Tom saw her action. 'Be quiet, Maggie,' he said, pushing her aside. Then: 'Aunt,' he said, looking straight at Mrs Glegg, 'if you think it's a disgrace to the family that our things should be sold, wouldn't it be better to prevent it? If you and my aunt Pullet think of leaving any money to me and Maggie, wouldn't it be better to give it now and save my mother from losing all her furniture?'

This speech was a fine piece of courage and good sense in a boy of sixteen. There was a silence for a few moments. Uncle Glegg was the first to speak.

'Well, young man, you understand a lot; but you must remember that your aunts get five per cent on their money, and they'd lose that if they did what you said.'

'I could work and pay that every year,' said Tom. 'I'd do anything to save my mother from losing her things.'

'Good!' said uncle Glegg.

'Oh, Mr Glegg,' said his wife angrily; 'I don't think you should be giving my money away. Sister Pullet, you may do

what you like, but why should I give my money away to people who've been wicked and wasteful?'

'I'm sorry for my sister and her children,' said Mrs Pullet, 'but it's no use for me to think of doing anything if you won't help.'

Maggie was filled with wild anger.

'Why do you come then?' she burst out, 'blaming us and scolding us, if you don't mean to do anything to help my poor mother—your own sister—when she's in trouble! Keep away from us, and don't come and find fault with my father. He was better than any of you; he was kind; he would have helped *you* if you'd been in trouble. Tom and I don't want to have any of your money. We'd rather not have it. We don't need you.'

'You haven't seen the end of your trouble with that child, Bessy,' said Mrs Pullet.

'That's enough. Don't let's waste time talking. Let's get to business,' said Mr Glegg.

A note for £300

'Why, there's Mrs Moss,' said Mrs Tulliver. 'The news must have reached her.'

Mrs Moss looked very different from the Dodson sisters as she entered the room in her poor, cheap dress. She seemed to take no notice of anyone except Tom. She went straight up to him and took him by the hand.

'Oh, my dear children,' she burst out, 'I'm a poor aunt to you, for I am one of those who take all and give nothing. How's my poor brother?'

'Dr Turnbull thinks he will get better,' said Maggie. 'Sit down, aunt Gritty.'

'Oh, my child, I feel torn in two,' said Mrs Moss. 'We've three hundred pounds of my brother's money, and you all want it, poor things!—and yet we must be sold up to pay it.'

'What madness!' said Mrs Glegg. 'He'd no right to lend his

money in that way; and I don't suppose there's any receipt or paper to show for it.'

'Yes,' replied Mrs Moss; 'my husband gave a note for the money.'

'Well,' said Mr Glegg gently, 'hasn't your husband any way of raising this money? It would be a fortune for these people now.'

'Oh, sir, you don't know what bad luck my husband has had on his farm. We've sold all the wheat, and we haven't paid the rent.'

'You've got to think of this, Mrs Moss,' said Mr Glegg, 'and it's right to warn you of it: if Mr Tulliver is sold up and he's got a note of your husband's for three hundred pounds, you'll be forced to pay it. So perhaps you should pay it now.'

'Uncle,' said Tom, looking up suddenly, 'I don't think it would be right for my aunt Moss to pay the money. It would be against my father's wishes. I remember quite well before I went to school to Mr Stelling, my father said to me one night, "I've always been good to my sister though she married against my will, and I've lent Moss money; but I should never think of making him pay it; I'd rather lose it all." And now my father is ill and not able to speak for himself—but I don't think anything ought to be done against his wishes.'

Mr Glegg looked surprised; then he said, 'Why, no, perhaps not, Tom. But if this is so, we shall have to destroy the note, you know.'

'Destroy a note!' said uncle Pullet. 'I'm not sure that isn't a crime.'

'I hope you'll help me to do it, uncle Glegg,' said Tom, taking no notice of uncle Pullet. 'I'm sure my father meant me to remember what he said that evening.'

Even Mrs Glegg secretly approved of Tom as he stood up so boldly; she felt that the Dodson blood was certainly speaking in him.

'Well,' said Mr Glegg, who had been thinking deeply, 'you

know we shall be taking the money away from the other people to whom your father also owes money. You are taking one man's dinner away to make another man's breakfast. You don't understand that, I suppose?'

'Yes, I do,' said Tom; 'but my father decided to give my aunt that money before he was in debt, and he had the right to do it then.'

'Well done, young man,' said uncle Glegg. 'Let's go and see if we can find the note.'

'It's in my father's room,' said Maggie.

Chapter 22
Tom seeks employment

Mr Deane

The days passed and Mr Tulliver slowly grew stronger, until at last the doctor was able to give hopes of a complete recovery.

While Mr Tulliver was slowly getting better, his fate and fortune were changing rapidly. By the beginning of the second week in January, the notices were out about the sale of his land and the mill; and soon afterwards the sale itself took place.

Both the mill and the land were sold to Wakem.

The new owner went round his property with Mr Glegg and Mr Deane. After visiting it and discussing the matter with these two gentlemen, Wakem told Mrs Tulliver that, if her husband recovered, he would be willing to keep him as manager of the business.

It was a dark, cold morning when Tom set off on his way to St Ogg to see his uncle Deane. He had decided that his uncle was the right person to ask for advice about getting some employment. Mr Deane had a great business, and he had risen in the world rapidly—and that was what Tom wanted to do.

By the time Tom had crossed the stone bridge over the Floss and was entering St Ogg, he was thinking that he would buy his father's land and mill again when he was rich enough. He would improve the house and live there and keep as many horses and dogs as he liked.

He woke from his dream of the future to a thorough consciousness of the present when he reached the offices of Deane & Co.

'This is Mr Deane's morning at the bank,' said the clerk, rather scornful that Tom did not know that. 'Mr Deane is never here on Thursday mornings.'

At the bank Tom was admitted into the private room where his uncle was. Mr Deane was at a large table looking over accounts. He glanced up as Tom entered, and put out his hand.

'Well, Tom,' he said, 'nothing new at home, I hope. How's your father?'

'He is much better, uncle,' said Tom. 'I want to speak to you, please, when you are free.'

'Sit down, sit down,' said Mr Deane, turning back to his accounts.

He continued to look over his accounts with his clerk for the next half-hour, and Tom began to wonder whether he would have to sit in this way until the bank closed for the day. Would his uncle give him a place in the bank? It would be very dull work to sit for ever listening to the loud *tick-tock, tick-tock* of the clock. He would prefer some other way of getting rich.

At last there was a change: his uncle took a pen and wrote something at the bottom of the page. 'Just go over to Mr Torry now, Mr Spence, please,' said Mr Deane.

The sound of the clock suddenly became less loud in Tom's ears.

'Well, Tom,' said Mr Deane, turning a little in his chair,

'what's the business, my boy? What's the business?'

'That depends'

'I hope you will excuse me for troubling you, uncle,' said Tom, rather red but speaking in a tone which had a certain proud independence in it; 'but I thought you were the best person to advise me what to do.'

'Ah,' said Mr Deane, looking at him with new attention, 'let's hear.'

'I want to get employment, uncle, so that I may earn some money,' said Tom.

'Employment?' said Mr Deane. 'Well—let me think—how old are you?' he asked, leaning back in his chair.

'I'm nearly seventeen,' said Tom, hoping that his uncle noticed how much beard he had.

'Well—people don't get much money at anything when they are only seventeen. You've had a lot of schooling, however; I suppose you're fairly good at accounts. Do you understand accounts?'

'No,' said Tom, with a slight tremble in his voice, 'but Mr Stelling says that my handwriting is good. This is some of my handwriting,' he added, laying on the table a piece of paper.

'Ah! That's good, that's good; but, you see, the best handwriting in the world will not get you a better place than a copying clerk, unless you know something about accounts; and copying clerks are cheap.'

'I want,' said Tom, 'to enter some business where I can get on quickly—a man's business where I should have to look after things—where, if I do well, I shall get the reward; and, if I don't—well, I shan't. I want to help my mother and sister.'

'Ah, young gentleman,' said Mr Deane, 'that's not as easy as it seems.'

'But didn't *you* get on in that way, uncle?' said Tom. 'I mean, didn't you rise from one place to another because you did well and worked hard.'

'Yes, yes,' said Mr Deane, spreading himself in his chair a little. 'But if I had successes, sir, it was because I made myself fit for them. If you want to slip into a round hole, you must make a ball of yourself—that's what it is.'

'Well, uncle,' said Tom, 'that's what I should like to do. Can't I get on in the same way?'

'In the same way?' said Mr Deane, eyeing Tom with quiet consideration. 'That depends on several things. It depends on what sort of material you are, and it depends on what sort of training you've had. That's where you are unfortunate. Your poor father didn't choose the right education for you. Latin is not any use to you.'

'No,' said Tom. 'But I don't see why the Latin need stop me. I shall soon forget it all. I had to do my lessons at school, but I always thought they would never be of any use to me afterwards.'

'Well,' answered Mr Deane, 'that doesn't alter what I was going to say. Your Latin may soon dry off you, but you will be only a bare stick after that. What do you know? You know nothing about accounts—nothing at all. You will have to begin right at the bottom, I must tell you, if you mean to get on in life. It's no use forgetting the education your father's been paying for, if you don't give yourself a new one.'

Tom bit his lips hard. He felt as if the tears were rising; but he would be a man!

'You want me to help you to find employment?' Mr Deane continued. 'Well, I am willing to do something for you.' Tom was going to speak but Mr Deane put up his hand. 'Hear what I've got to say. You don't want to be a copying clerk. You don't want to stand behind a desk and gaze at your ink and paper all day. No! Now the best chance for you is to take a place in the store-house by the river-side where the ships are unloaded. You will learn the smell of things there—but you won't like that, I suppose? You'll have to stand out in the open when it is cold and wet, and be knocked about by rough fellows; but you're too fine a gentleman for that, I suppose?' Mr Deane paused and looked hard at Tom.

'I will do what's best for me in the end, sir,' said Tom. 'I don't mind how unpleasant it is. I had better set about learning accounts immediately, hadn't I, uncle?' he added.

'Well done, Tom, well done!' said Mr Deane. 'That's the right spirit. I never refuse to help anyone if they have made up their minds to help themselves.'

'What did uncle Deane say?' asked Maggie, putting her arm through Tom's as he was warming himself by the kitchen fire. 'Did he say that he would give you some employment?'

'He seemed to think that I couldn't have a very good place,' said Tom. 'He said I was too young.'

'But didn't he speak kindly, Tom?'

'He said I must set about learning accounts and those things,' answered Tom. 'He seems to think I'm useless.'

'Accounts?' said Maggie. 'Oh, I can teach you that. I learnt them with Lucy at school.'

Chapter 23
Something is written in the Bible

Mr Tulliver gets up

Two months had passed, and Mr Tulliver was now strong enough to leave his bed. He sat down to rest after dressing. Maggie and Tom were waiting for him, when Luke entered and asked if he could help the master to get downstairs.

'Yes, yes, Luke,' said Mr Tulliver. 'But wait a bit—sit down'—he pointed his stick towards a chair.

'How is the water now, eh, Luke?' said Mr Tulliver. 'No more trouble with Dix, eh?'

'No, sir, it's all right.'

'It's a long time since you had that quarrel with Dix, father,' said Tom. 'I remember you talking about it before I went to school at Mr Stelling's. I've been at school three years; don't you remember?'

Mr Tulliver leant back in his chair. His face lost the childlike look as a rush of new memories came into his mind.

'Yes, yes,' he said after a minute or two, 'I've paid a lot of money. I was determined my son should have a good education. I had none myself and I felt the lack of it. If Wakem...'

He stopped. The thought of Wakem brought a new idea into his mind. He began to feel in the pocket of his coat. Then he turned to Tom and said in his old sharp way, 'Where have they put Gore's letter?'

'You know what there is in the letter, father?' said Tom as he gave it to him.

'Of course I do,' said Mr Tulliver rather angrily. 'And it doesn't matter. If Furley can't take the property, somebody else can. But I must go and see Gore about it; he's expecting me. Tell them to get ready the horse.'

'No, dear father,' cried Maggie. 'It's a long time since all that. Everything is changed.'

Mr Tulliver looked at them questioningly.

'Yes, father,' said Tom. 'Everything is settled for the present about the mill and the land and the debts.'

'You would have paid everybody if you could, sir,' said Luke. 'That's what I said to Master Tom.'

Mr Tulliver promises to make amends

'Paid everybody?' said Mr Tulliver '—*would* have paid everybody? Why.... Have they—sold me up?'

'Oh, father, dear father,' said Maggie, 'Tom will pay them all. He says he will, when he is a man.'

She saw her father's lips tremble.

'Yes, my little girl,' he said, and his voice trembled too, 'but I shall never live twice over.'

'Perhaps you will live to see me pay everybody, father,' said Tom.

His father looked up at him. 'You're only seventeen, Tom,' he said. 'It's an uphill fight for you—but you mustn't blame your father. The rascals have been too clever for him.'

He paused.

'So they've sold me up?' he repeated more calmly.

'You mustn't be surprised to see the room look very bare downstairs,' said Maggie. 'But there's your chair and desk; they're not gone.'

'Let's go. Help me down, Luke,' said Mr Tulliver.

He paused just inside the door of the sitting-room and looked at all the bare places which for him were filled with shadows of departed objects—the daily companions of his life.

'Ah,' he said slowly, moving towards his chair, 'they've sold me up.'

He sat down, and then looked round again.

'They've left the big Bible,' he said. 'It has got everything written in it—when I was born—and married. . . . Bring it to me, Tom.'

Mrs Tulliver entered the room, but stood in speechless surprise to find her husband downstairs already, and with the great Bible opened in front of him.

'Ah,' he said. 'Margaret Beaton—that was my mother . . . Elizabeth Dodson. It's eighteen years since I married her.'

'Eighteen years last March,' said Mrs Tulliver, going to his side and looking at the page.

Her husband fixed his eyes on her face.

'Poor Bessy,' he said. 'You were a pretty girl then—everybody said so—and I used to think that you kept your good looks well; but this trouble has made you look older. Don't hate me for it.'

'Of course not. But I never thought it would be as bad as this,' said poor Mrs Tulliver.

'Don't say that, Bessy,' said Mr Tulliver. 'If there is anything

I can do to make you amends, I swear I will do it.'

'Then we might stay here so that I might be near my own sisters; but we won't because you hate Wakem so much.'

'Mother,' said Tom severely, 'this is not the time to talk about that!'

'Leave her alone,' said Mr Tulliver. 'Say what you mean, Bessy.'

'The mill and the land all belong to Wakem. He says that you may stay here and that he'll pay you thirty shillings a week to manage the business. Where else can we go? We must go into one of the cottages in the village—and all because you hate Wakem!'

Mr Tulliver had sunk back in his chair trembling.

'You may do what you like with me, Bessy,' he said at last in a low voice. 'It was I who made you poor. This world has been too difficult for me.'

He remained in silent thought for several minutes.

Then he looked up. 'Tom!' he said sharply; 'Tom! sit down here. I have got something for you to write in the Bible.'

Tom writes a promise

The three others looked at Mr Tulliver, wondering what this might mean. He began to speak slowly, looking first at his wife.

'I have made up my mind, Bessy: I swore to you to do what I could to make amends; and I'll do it. I'll stop in the old place, and I'll serve under Wakem; and I'll serve him like an honest man. I'll serve him as honestly as if he were not a rascal. I *am* an honest man—though I shall hang my head in shame for the rest of my life.'

He paused and looked on the ground. Then, suddenly raising his head, he said in a louder and deeper voice:

'But I won't forgive him! I won't forgive him! I wish he may be punished with shame until his own son would like to forget him! And you remember this, Tom—you must never forgive him either, if you mean to be my son. Perhaps a time will come when you may make him feel—feel some of the shame that I am feeling now. Now write; write it in the Bible.'

'Oh, father, what?' said Maggie, sinking down by his knee, pale and trembling. 'It's wicked to curse and bear hatred!'

'It isn't wicked, I tell you,' said her father fiercely. 'It's wicked that rascals should succeed. The devil helps them. Do as I tell you, Tom. Write!'

'What am I to write?'

'Write that your father, Edward Tulliver, agreed to work for John Wakem, the man who had ruined him, because he had promised his wife to make her amends, and because he wanted to die in the old place where he was born and where his father was born. And then write: "But I don't forgive Wakem, and, though I'll serve him honestly, I hope that evil may come to him." Write that!'

There was a dead silence as Tom's pen moved along the paper. Mrs Tulliver gazed out of frightened eyes and Maggie trembled like a leaf.

'Now let me hear what you have written,' said Mr Tulliver.

Tom read aloud, slowly.

'Now write—' said Mr Tulliver— 'write "I, Thomas Tulliver, his son, will remember what Wakem has done to my father and I will make him and his family suffer, if ever the chance comes," and sign your name, "Thomas Tulliver".'

'Oh, no, father; dear father,' cried Maggie, breathless with fear; 'you shouldn't make Tom write that.'

'Be quiet, Maggie,' said Tom. 'I *shall* write it.'

Chapter 24
Womanhood

Maggie was now on the edge of womanhood, when the mind is ordinarily full of new hopes, new dreams, new joys; yet this season of great change was to her the hardest time of all her life.

In the first shock of trouble it is easy to be brave, because pain is an excitement which helps us to call up our strength. It is in the slow, changed life that follows, in the time when day follows day with unexpected sameness, that despair threatens us.

It was now that Maggie reached the time when she had greatest need of strength.

Tom went every morning to his business at Mr Deane's, and became more and more silent in the short time when he was at home in the evening: he thought of nothing but his dreams —his dreams of repairing the disaster.

Poor Mrs Tulliver would never again work quietly and contentedly in the house as in the old days. How could she? All her little treasures were taken away; all her little hopes and plans were gone. Why had this happened to her? It was pitiful to see this once beautiful woman getting thinner and more worn by restlessness of mind and of body. She refused to sit down and rest. She would not let Maggie do any of the heaviest or dirty work, and became angry when Maggie tried to do it instead of her. 'Leave it, dear; your hands'll get hard. It's your mother's duty to do that.'

The restless condition of her mother was less painful to Maggie than her father's silent despair. There were hard lines about his mouth, and his dull eye never brightened with any eagerness or joy. He never spent time away from home: he hurried back from the market; he refused all invitations to stay and talk, as in old times, in the houses where he called on business. He could not settle down to his new life. His pride was hurt by everything which was said to him. Even the days on which Wakem came to ride round the land and to enquire into the business were not so black to him as those market days on which he had to meet people to whom he still owed money. He was now bending all his thoughts and efforts to one purpose—payment of those debts. Mrs Tulliver could not be careful enough in their food; he would eat nothing himself that was not the very cheapest. Tom, though he hated his father's silent despair and the sadness of the home, fully shared his father's feelings about paying off the debts. He brought his money month by month and gave it to his father to put in the tin box which held the savings. The little store of coins in the tin box seemed to be the only sight that brought a faint sign of pleasure into Mr Tulliver's eyes.

Yet Mr Tulliver still kept the old feeling towards his 'little girl'. He needed her presence, although it did not seem to cheer him.

In the evenings Maggie took her sewing and sat on a low chair by her father's knee.

As she bent over her sewing, Maggie was a sight that anyone might have been pleased to look at. The new inward life of her soul shone out in her face with a soft, tender light. Her mother felt the change in her, and wondered that Maggie 'should be growing up so well'. She was getting fond of her tall, dark girl.

As she said to her husband, 'Our daughter's getting quite a beautiful girl, isn't she, Mr Tulliver?'

'I knew what she'd be,' was the reply; 'it's nothing new to me. But it's a pity she's not made of commoner stuff. She'll be thrown away, I'm afraid: there'll be nobody to marry her who is fit for her.'

Maggie's graces of mind and body added to his grief.

Chapter 25
In the Red Deeps

Maggie sees Philip again

Maggie was sitting at the window of her bedroom when she saw Mr Wakem entering the yard as usual on his fine black horse. But he was not alone as usual; someone was with him—someone riding a fine grey horse. It was Philip Wakem. He saw her and raised his hat, and his father looked sharply round.

Maggie did not go downstairs, because Mr Wakem sometimes came in and inspected the accounts, and she felt that the meeting with Philip would lose all its pleasure in the presence of the two fathers. Some day, perhaps, she would see him, and they would shake hands, and she would tell him that she remembered his goodness to Tom; but they could never be friends any more. She thought, besides, that Philip himself might be altered by his life abroad. He might have become quite different, and really not want her to speak to him now. And yet his face was wonderfully little changed; it was only a larger, more manly, copy of the pale boy's face with the grey eyes and the boyish, waving hair; and there was the old deformity to awaken the old pity. Maggie felt she really would like to say a few words to him. She wondered if he remembered how he used to like her eyes; and she half turned towards the square looking-glass hanging on the wall; then checked herself and took up her sewing.

Some minutes later she saw Philip and his father returning along the road.

One of Maggie's favourite walks was to a spot called 'The Red Deeps', which lay beyond the hill south of Dorlcote Mill. Men had once taken building stone from the hillside there, but it was now overgrown with trees. Grass had covered the wounded earth. There she often sat in a grassy hollow under the shadow of a branching tree.

A few days after Philip Wakem's visit to the mill, Maggie

was in the Deeps, calmly enjoying the free air. She looked up at the old trees, and thought that those broken ends of branches were records of past storms which had only made the red trunks climb higher.

While her eyes were still turned upwards, she became conscious of a moving shadow cast by the evening sun on the grassy path in front of her. Philip Wakem was there. He came forward to her and put out his hand.

'You surprised me,' said Maggie, smiling. 'I never meet anyone here. How did you happen to be walking here?'

'I came to meet you,' said Philip. 'I wanted to see you very much. I waited a long time yesterday on the bank near your house to see if you would come out; but you never came. I went again today, and saw the path you took, and kept you in sight. I hope you aren't angry with me.'

'No,' said Maggie with simple seriousness. 'I'm very glad you came. I wanted to have an opportunity of speaking to you; but I was not sure that you would remember us so well as we remember you.'

'I can't believe that you have thought about me so much as I have thought about you,' said Philip. 'When I was away, I made a picture of you as you looked that morning in the study when you said you would not forget me.'

Philip drew a small case from his pocket and opened it. It was a picture Philip had drawn of her long ago at Mr Stelling's house. Maggie saw herself leaning on the table, with her black hair hanging down behind her ears, looking into space with strange, dreamy eyes.

'Oh,' said Maggie, 'what a queer little girl I was.—Perhaps I am now,' she added after a little pause. 'Am I like what you expected me to be?'

Philip looked into her eyes. 'No, Maggie,' he said quietly. 'You are much more beautiful than I thought you would be.'

She stood up and walked onward a few steps, and Philip walked by her side, watching her face. They left the group of trees and came to a green hollow surrounded by wild rose bushes. She stood still and looked at Philip.

'I wish we could have been friends; but I can't keep anything I used to love when I was little. The old books went, and Tom is different—and my father. I must lose everything that I cared for when I was a child—and you too. That was why I wanted to speak to you. If I behave as if I had forgotten all about you, you must understand...'

There was a deepening expression of pain on Philip's face.

'I know. I see what you mean,' he said. 'But is it right to sacrifice everything to other people's unreasonable feelings?'

'I don't know,' said Maggie thoughtfully; 'but I'm quite sure that I don't want to do anything which might make my father's life harder for him.'

'Would it make his life harder if we saw each other sometimes?' said Philip.

'He feels so strongly about some things,' said Maggie. 'I'm sure he wouldn't like it. He's not at all happy.'

'Nor am I happy,' said Philip. '*I* am not happy.'

'Why?' asked Maggie very gently.

'We know that some things are beautiful and good,' he replied; 'and we hunger for them; but I can't have them. There are things that I long for, things that other men have—that will never be mine. My life will have nothing great or beautiful in it; and I would rather not have lived. Yet I should be content to live if you would let me see you sometimes. I have no other friend to whom I can tell everything—no one who cares about me. If I could only see you occasionally, if you would let me talk to you a little, if we might always be friends in heart and help each other—then I might be glad of life.'

'But how can I see you, Philip?' said Maggie.

'If you would let me see you here sometimes, walk with you here—that could harm no one's happiness, and it would sweeten my life. And if there is any hatred between those who belong to us, oughtn't we to try to end it by our friendship, and by our influence heal the wounds that have been made in the past?'

Maggie was silent. Opposing forces battled in her mind.

'I can't say either "yes" or "no",' she said at last, turning round and walking towards the way she had come. 'I must wait, in case I decide wrongly.'

'May I come again then—tomorrow—or the next day—or next week? Tell me when; or, if you can't tell me, I will come as often as I can until I see you.'

'I think it must be that,' said Maggie, 'because I can't be quite certain when I can come.' She hastened forward.

'Don't hurry away from me without saying good-bye, Maggie,' said Philip, as they reached the end of the path.

She paused.

'Goodbye,' she said, holding out her hand to him.

They stood looking at each other in silence, her hand in his.

Then she looked round: 'Oh, the sun is setting! I have been too long away. Goodbye.'

Chapter 26
A year later

Tom does well

A year has passed since the scene which we have just described, and in that year Tom has been very successful.

One might have expected that Tom would succeed: his strong will, his pride, his desire to repair the disasters of the past—all gave him a strength to overcome all difficulties. Mr Deane watched him closely and soon began to have high hopes of him and to be proud that he had brought into his business a young fellow who appeared to be made of such good stuff.

Tom soon understood Mr Deane's real kindness in placing him in the store-house first. He learned so much there that, after a short time, he was given the task of buying various materials. His wages were raised; but, more than that, he was allowed to do some little trading for himself. He borrowed from his uncle Glegg a small amount of money which quickly became greater, and he thought that he might soon be able to buy back the old mill.

A kiss

It is an afternoon in early April. Maggie walked quickly along the path towards her favourite spot. There was a more eager, enquiring look in her eyes than there was last June, and there was a little smile on her lips as if she had something amusing to say to the right hearer.

The hearer soon appeared.

'Thank you for lending me this book,' said Maggie. 'But I didn't finish it, and I'm not going to finish it. I am determined not to read any more books where the fair-haired women get all the happiness.'

'I wonder,' said Philip, 'if you would think the same if *you* had. . .'

'Philip,' said Maggie, looking hurt, 'that is not nice of you. The reason is that I always care most about the unhappy people in books. If the fair-haired girl were miserable, I should like her best. I always take the side of the person who suffers in the stories.'

'Then could you—' asked Philip anxiously—'could you take the side of a man who has been marked from childhood for a peculiar kind of suffering, a man to whom you are the one bright star of his life, who has loved you so entirely that he feels it happiness enough if you let him see you at rare moments. . .'

Philip paused, with a sudden fear in case his confession cut short this very happiness—a fear which had kept his love unspoken through all these long months. Maggie was silent; she sat down on a fallen tree trunk, and Philip sat beside her. 'Do you love me?' he dared to ask at last.

Her eyes met Philip's, liquid and beautiful with love. 'I think I could hardly love anyone better,' she said. And she kissed him, almost as simply and quietly as she had done when she was twelve years old.

Tom is cruel

There was a sound in the bushes. They turned and saw Tom.

'You call yourself a man and a gentleman!' he cried in a voice of scorn, as soon as Philip had risen.

'What do you mean?' answered Philip quietly.

'Mean? Stand further away from me—or I might strike you —and I'll tell you what I mean. I mean taking advantage of a young girl's foolishness to hold secret meetings with her. I mean attempting to bring shame on my family which has a good and honest name.'

'I have *not* done that!' cried Philip fiercely. 'I seek nothing but your sister's happiness: she is dearer to me than she is to you. I honour her more than you can ever honour her—than you have ever honoured her—and I would give up my life for her.'

Tom looked at him with hatred. 'Do you pretend that you have any right to tell her of your love—even if you had been a fit husband for her? You know that neither her father nor your father would ever agree to a marriage between you. And yet you...'

'Can't you understand what I feel for your sister?' cried Philip.

'What I want *you* to understand,' answered Tom, 'is that if you dare to make the least attempt to come near her, or write to her, or keep the slightest hold on her mind, your miserable, deformed body won't protect you. I'll beat you. I'll hold you up to public scorn—and who wouldn't laugh at the idea of *your* turning lover!'

He seized Maggie's arm as he spoke and dragged her away.

At last, when they were some distance from the place, with a violent effort Maggie drew her arm away. Her anger burst out: 'Don't suppose that I'm obeying you because you're right, Tom! I despise the feelings you have shown in speaking to Philip. I hate your insults to him for his deformity. You have been blaming and despising other people all your life—you have always been so sure that you yourself are right. It's because you haven't a mind large enough to see that there's anything better than your own behaviour and your own low aims. I hate you!'

Chapter 27
A hard-won triumph

Three weeks have passed. It is the month of May, and Dorlcote Mill is at its prettiest moment in all the year.

Tom Tulliver came home a little earlier than usual in the evening, and as he passed over the bridge he looked with the old deep-rooted affection at the solid, red-brick house which always seemed cheerful and inviting outside, even though inside the rooms were bare and the hearts were sad. As he looked at his home, his firm step became quicker, and at the corner of his mouth there was the suggestion of a smile.

Mr Tulliver was in his armchair, tired after a long ride; Maggie was bending over her sewing, and her mother was making tea. They all looked up with surprise as he entered.

'Why, what's the matter, Tom?' said his father. 'You're back earlier than usual.'

'Oh, there was nothing more for me to do; so I came away. Well, mother!' He went up to his mother and kissed her—a sign of unusual good temper with him. But to Maggie he said nothing—hardly a word or look had passed between them during the last three weeks.

'Father,' said Tom, when they had finished tea, 'do you know exactly how much money there is in the tin box?'

'Only one hundred and ninety-three pounds,' said Mr Tulliver. 'You've brought me less money lately; young fellows like to have their own way with their money. But I didn't do as I liked with my money when I was your age.' He spoke with a mixture of fear and discontent.

'Are you quite sure that is the amount, father?' said Tom. 'I wish you would take the trouble to fetch the tin box down. I think you have perhaps made a mistake.'

'How could I make a mistake?' said his father sharply. 'I've counted it often enough; but I'll fetch it if you won't believe me.' Mr Tulliver liked fetching the tin box and counting the money. It was the only thing in his sad life which seemed to give him any pleasure.

'Don't go out of the room, mother,' said Tom, as he saw her preparing to carry the tea-things away.

'And isn't Maggie to go?' said Mrs Tulliver. 'Someone has got to take away these things.'

'She can do just as she likes,' said Tom coldly.

Tom came to the corner of the table near his father when the tin box was set down and opened. The red evening light shone on their faces, showing up a look of sad weariness in the father's face and in Tom's a look of scarcely hidden joy. The mother and Maggie sat at the other end of the table. Mrs Tulliver looked quietly patient, expecting nothing; but Maggie's heart was beating violently.

Mr Tulliver counted out the money and set it in order on the table. Then he glanced sharply at Tom. 'There now! you see, I was right.' He paused, looking at the money despairingly. 'But we need more than three hundred pounds more before I can pay my debts. It will be a long time before I can save that. This world has been too difficult for me. It has taken four years to save this amount, and I don't suppose I shall live for another four years. . . . I must trust you to pay them—if you still mean to do it now that you're growing up.' He looked up in Tom's face doubtfully.

'No, father,' said Tom; 'you shall live to see all the debts paid. You shall pay them with your own hand.' There was in his voice something more than a mere expression of hope. An electric shock seemed to pass through Mr Tulliver, and he kept his eyes fixed on Tom with a look of eager enquiry.

Tom paused a little before he went on. 'Some time ago my uncle Glegg lent me a little money to trade with, and that has succeeded. It has succeeded so well that I have the money to pay all your debts.'

His mother's arms were around his neck as soon as the last words were out: 'Oh, my boy, I knew you'd make everything right again when you became a man.'

But his father was silent—too full of emotion to speak. Then suddenly the grey-haired man burst into loud sobs. At last he looked up at his wife and said in a gentle voice, 'Bessy, you must come and kiss me now; our son has made you amends.'

She kissed him, and he held her hand for a minute; then his thoughts went back to the money.

'I wish you'd brought me the money to look at, Tom,' he said, fingering the coins on the table. 'I should have felt surer.'

'You shall see it tomorrow, father,' said Tom. 'My uncle Deane has arranged a meeting of all those to whom you owe money tomorrow at the hotel; and he has ordered a dinner for them at two o'clock. There was a notice about it in the paper on Saturday.'

'Then Wakem knows of it!' said Mr Tulliver, his eye bright with triumph. 'He knows it, and I shan't be under Wakem's thumb any longer. Oh, Wakem would be glad to have a son like mine—a fine, straight fellow—instead of that poor, deformed creature. You'll do well in the world, my boy, and perhaps you will see the day when Wakem and his son will be below you. Shake hands with me, my boy,' he said suddenly, putting out his hand. 'It's a great thing when a man can be proud that he has got a good son.'

It was long before Mr Tulliver got to sleep that night; and the sleep, when it came, was filled with restless dreams. At half-past five in the morning he alarmed Mrs Tulliver by sitting up in bed with a shout.

'What's the matter?' said his wife.

He looked round in a wondering way at the walls of the bedroom.

'What's the matter?' he repeated. 'Ah, I was dreaming... Did I make a noise?...I—I thought I had got hold of him in my hands.'

Chapter 28
A day of vengeance

Wakem

The next day, when Mr Tulliver was at table in the hotel, his eye was bright, and he looked more like the proud, warm-hearted Tulliver of old times. After the meal he made a speech with his old firmness, talking about 'honest men' and 'rascals', and the triumph which had been won by hard efforts and the aid of a good son. The party ended quietly at five o'clock.

Tom remained at St Ogg to attend to some business, but Mr Tulliver mounted his horse to go home and to describe these great events to Bessy and his 'little girl'. He looked excited, not because of the good dinner, but because of a sense of triumph. He did not ride through any back street today, but passed slowly with his head held high along the main road all the way to the bridge. Why did he not happen to meet

Wakem? It annoyed him that he did not meet Wakem; and this small disappointment planted a seed of anger in his mind. Perhaps Wakem had gone out of town today on purpose to avoid seeing or hearing anything of an honourable action: anything honourable *would* be unpleasant to Wakem, Mr Tulliver thought. 'If I met him now, I would look straight at him, and the rascal would perhaps not be so cool and so certain of himself as he usually is. Before long, he'll know that an honest man is not going to serve *him* any longer. Wakem won't use *my* honesty to fill *his* pocket, which is already too full of dishonest gains.'

Still in this angry state of mind, Mr Tulliver approached the gates of Dorlcote Mill. As he came near them he saw a well-known figure coming out on a fine black horse. They met about fifty yards from the gates.

'Tulliver!' said Wakem in a sharper tone than usual, 'what a stupid thing you've done, spreading those hard masses of earth on the upper field; but you men will never learn how to manage a farm properly.'

'Oh,' said Tulliver, his rage boiling up inside him; 'get somebody else to manage your farm then!—somebody who will ask *you* to teach him!'

'You've been drinking, I suppose,' said Wakem.

'No, I've not been drinking,' said Tulliver. 'I don't need wine to help me to decide that I'll no longer serve under a rascal.'

'Very well,' said Wakem, 'you can go tomorrow; but be silent and let me pass'—for Tulliver had turned his horse across the road so that Wakem could not get past.

'No, I shan't let you pass,' said Tulliver. 'I shall tell you what I think of you first. You're too big a rascal to get hanged! You're...'

'Let me pass, you stupid fool, or I'll ride over you.'

Mr Tulliver made a rush forward, raising his whip. Wakem's horse was frightened, and threw his rider from the saddle. Before he could rise, Tulliver had sprung off his horse too. The sight of the long-hated enemy down on the ground and in his power threw him into a madness of triumphant vengeance. He rushed at Wakem and beat him fiercely with his riding whip. Wakem shouted for help, but no help came. His mad anger seemed to give Tulliver unnatural strength. He held Wakem down on the ground and beat him.

A woman's scream was heard, and the cry of 'Father! Father!'

The blows stopped.

'Leave me alone! Go away!' cried Tulliver. But he was not speaking to Wakem.

The lawyer looked up and saw that Tulliver's arms were held by a girl.

'Father, come away...' cried Maggie, still holding his arms, while Mrs Tulliver stood by in silence, shaking with fear. And then Maggie realised that her father was beginning to hold on to her and lean on her.

'I feel ill—faint,' he said. 'Help me in, Bessy. I've got a pain in the head.' He walked in slowly, helped by his wife and daughter, and fell into his chair. His face was deathly pale and his hand was cold.

'We must send for the doctor,' said Mrs Tulliver.

'Doctor,' he whispered, 'no—no doctor. It's my head—that's all. Help me to bed.'

Death

Tom, tired out by his busy day, had soon fallen asleep. It seemed to him as if he had only just come to bed when he was woken by his mother in the grey light of early morning.

'My boy, you must get up this minute. I've sent for the doctor, and your father wants you and Maggie to come to him. He has been very ill all night with a pain in his head. Then suddenly he said, "Bessy, fetch the boy and girl; tell them to hurry."'

Maggie and Tom reached their father's room almost at the same moment. He was watching for them with an expression of pain on his face. Maggie was at the bedside first, but her father's glance was towards Tom, who came and stood next to her.

'Tom, my boy, I know that I shan't get up again. . . . This world has been too difficult for me; but you've done what you could to make things right. Shake hands with me again, my son, before I go away from you.'

The father and son took each other's hands for an instant.

'There's your mother—you'll try to make her amends, all you can, for my bad luck . . . And there's my little girl . . .'

The father turned his eyes on Maggie with an eager look.

'Kiss me, Maggie. Don't grieve, my little girl. There will be someone who'll love you and stand up for you. . . . Come, Bessy . . .'

He looked away from them and lay silent for some minutes. The morning light was growing clearer and they could see the heaviness gathering in his face and the dullness in his eyes.

'I had my turn,' he whispered. 'I beat him. That was only fair. I never wanted anything that wasn't fair.'

'But, father, dear father,' said Maggie, 'you forgive him—you forgive everyone now?'

He didn't move his eyes to look at her, but he said, 'No, my girl, I don't forgive him. I don't forgive rascals.'

His voice became thicker. He moved his lips again and again, struggling to speak.

And then there came from him some broken words—'This world . . . too difficult . . . honest man . . . difficult . . .'

The loud, hard breathing stopped. Silence—and rest.

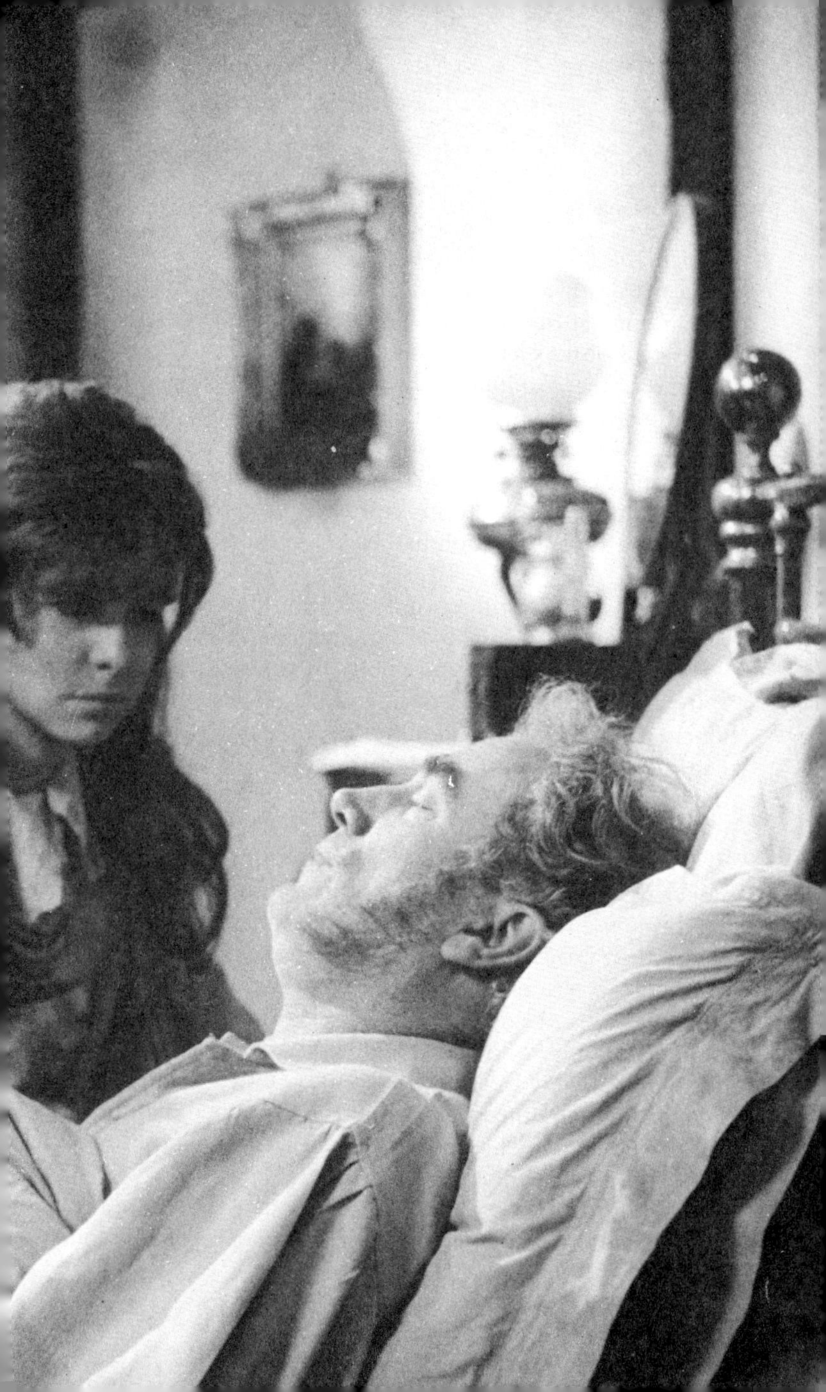

Chapter 29
Flood

Despair

After the death of her father, it was not possible for Maggie to remain long at the old mill. To meet her brother every day, to bear his bitter silences was more than her heart could suffer. She stayed there so long as she felt she could help her mother to settle down to the changed life; but she could not do much for her. After a few unbearable weeks, during which Tom's anger and disapproval seemed to increase rather than to grow less, she decided at last to move into St Ogg to the home of Mrs Jakin, whose son Bob had been a great friend in their childhood.

Mr Wakem was still seriously ill. From Philip she had received one short, heartbroken letter: then silence.

There seemed in the future no hope for her, no forgiveness.

It was the second week of June. Maggie was sitting in her lonely room on the ground floor of Mrs Jakin's house, battling with her regrets and fears. It was past midnight, and the rain was beating heavily against the window, driven by the pitiless rushing wind.

The week before, there had been continuous rain on the upper part of the river. And now for the last two days the rain on this lower course of the river had never stopped. Old men shook their heads and talked of sixty years ago, when the same sort of weather brought on great floods which swept the bridge away and brought great misery to the town. But the younger people, who had seen several small floods, thought the old men were foolish. Mrs Jakin regretted their having taken a house by the river-side; but Bob replied that, being by the river-side, they had boats—which were the most lucky of possessions in case of a flood.

But now, both the careless and the fearful were sleeping in their beds, since it was past midnight—all except some lonely watchers such as Maggie. She sat, unconscious of how the hours were going, not trying to rest; she could see no rest for her in the future.

At last, with a cry of despair, she fell on her knees beside the table. Her soul went out to the Unseen Pity that would be with her to the end: 'Oh, God,' she cried, 'if my life is to be long, let me live to bless and comfort those whom I love.'

She felt something strange—a feeling of cold about her knees and feet. It was water flowing under her. She stood up: the stream was flowing under the door that led into the passage. It was the flood!

The fierce emotions which had torn her for the last few hours seemed to have left a great calm in her. Without a word or cry, she took her candle and hurried upstairs to Bob Jakin's room. The door was half open. She went in and shook him by the shoulder.

'Bob, the flood has come! It's in the house! We must make the boats safe.'

Alone on the flood

While Bob put on his clothes, she hurried down again to see if the waters were rising fast. She saw that the last step of the stairs was already under water. While she was looking, something struck the window with a fearful crash, and sent the glass and the wooden frame inwards in pieces. And the water came pouring in after it.

'It's the boat!' cried Maggie. 'Bob, come down and get the boats!'

Without a moment's fear she pushed her way through the water, which was rising fast to her knees, climbed through the window and crept into the boat. Bob was not long after her. He came hurrying down with a lamp in his hand.

'Oh, they're both here, both the boats!' said Bob, as he got into the one in which Maggie was. 'It's wonderful that this rope hasn't broken.'

He climbed into the other boat and began to untie the rope —without thinking of the danger for Maggie.

'The water's rising so fast,' he said, 'that I'm afraid it will be in at the upper rooms before long; the house is so low. I'd like to get my mother and sister into the boat if I can. . . . But what about you?' he exclaimed suddenly, turning the light of his lamp on Maggie as she stood there in the rain, the water streaming from her black hair.

Maggie had no time to answer, for a new rush of water swept along the line of the house and drove both the boats out into the middle of the river. . .

In the first moments Maggie felt nothing—thought of nothing. She seemed suddenly to have passed away from the life which she had been dreading. It was like death without its pain.

She was alone in the darkness with God.

Chapter 30
The waters of comfort

Darkness

The whole thing had been so rapid—so dreamlike, that the ordinary threads of thought were broken. Maggie sank down on the seat of the boat, and for a long time had no clear idea of her position.

The first thing that wakened her to fuller consciousness was a realisation that the darkness was divided by the faintest line separating the black curtain of overhanging sky from the great stretch of water below. She had been driven out on the flood —that dreadful disaster of which her father used to talk—that thing which made her childhood dreams terrible. And with that thought there rushed into her mind a vision of the old home, and Tom, and her mother.

'Oh, God! Where am I? Which is the way home?' she cried

out. What was happening to them at the mill? The flood had once nearly destroyed it. They might be in danger—in distress: her mother and her brother alone there where no one could help them! Her whole soul was filled with that thought. She saw the long-loved faces looking for aid into the darkness, and finding none.

She was floating now on smooth water—perhaps far away over the flooded fields. She tried to see through the wall of darkness to get some idea of where she was—to find some faint suggestion of the way to her old home.

There was a gradual uplifting of the cloudy sky, and the blackness below slowly formed itself into dimly seen shapes. Yes—she must be out in the fields. Those were the tops of the hedges. Which way was the river? Looking behind her, she saw a line of black trees: looking ahead, there were none: therefore the river was ahead of her. She began to row the boat forward with the energy of awakening hope. First light seemed to advance more swiftly now that she was in action. She could see the poor cattle crowding on a little hill upstanding above the flood.

Half-light

Onward she rowed in the growing half-light. Her wet clothes hung around her and the wind whipped her wet hair into her face. But she was hardly conscious of any bodily feelings except a sense of strength given to her by strong emotion. Along with a sense of danger and possible risk for the loved ones at the old home, there was a half-conscious sense of peace with her brother. What quarrel, what anger, what disbelief, can remain in the presence of a great disaster? Dimly Maggie felt this; and a great love towards her brother swept away all the effects of cruel misunderstanding, leaving only the deep, underlying, unshakable memories of early union.

But now there was a large, dark mass in the distance, and Maggie could see the current of the river near to her. That dark mass must be—yes, it was St Ogg. Now she knew which way to look for the well-known trees—and, above them, the old roof: but there was no colour, no shape yet; all was faint and dim.

More and more the needed strength seemed to come to her, as if her life were a stored-up force that was being spent in this hour, unneeded for any future time.

She must get her boat into the current of the Floss. Otherwise she would never be able to pass the Ripple and approach the house. This was the thought that came to her—but then she might be carried too far down and be unable to get her boat out of the current again. For the first time, she had a clear idea of danger; but there was no moment of doubt. She floated into the current. Swiftly she went on now without effort. More and more clearly, in the lessening distance and the growing light, she began to see the objects that she knew must be the well-known trees and roofs. And that rushing, muddy current—that must be the strangely altered Ripple.

Great God! There were floating masses in it that might dash against her boat and end her life too soon. What were those masses?

'Here's Maggie'

Maggie's heart began to beat in terror: she sat helpless, dimly conscious that she was being floated along—more clearly conscious of the possible disaster.

But the fear passed—passed as she reached the store-houses of St Ogg. The mouth of the Ripple was behind her: *now* she must use all her skill and power to get the boat out of the current. With new determination she began to row. But, as the river neared the sea, the current became swifter, and she was carried along beyond the bridge.

She could hear shouts from the windows overlooking the river, as if the people were calling to her. It was not till she had passed on nearly to Tofton that she could get the boat clear of the current. Then she rowed with all her strength across the flooded fields back towards the mill. The daylight was stronger now: as she approached the Dorlcote fields she could see the colours of the trees—how deep they stood in the water!—and the roof of the mill—where was it? Those heavy masses hurrying down the Ripple—what did they mean? But no, it was not the house—the house stood firm. The water was above the lower windows, but it was still firm—or was it broken at the end?

With breathless joy she knew that she was there at last—joy that overcame all distress. She neared the front of the house. At first she heard no sound: she saw no object moving. Her boat was on a level with the upstairs window. She called out as loudly as she could:

'Tom, where are you? Mother, where are you? Here's Maggie.'

Soon from the window of that little room under the roof she heard Tom's voice: 'Who is it? Have you brought a boat?'

'It's Maggie, Tom. It's Maggie. Where's mother?'

'She's not here. She went to aunt Pullet's the day before yesterday. I'll come down to the lower window.'

'Alone, Maggie?' said Tom in a voice of deep astonishment as he opened the window on a level with the boat.

'Yes, Tom. Get in quickly. Is there no one else?'

'No,' said Tom, stepping into the boat. 'I'm afraid Luke is drowned. He was carried down, I think, when part of the mill fell. I've shouted again and again and there's been no answer. Let me row, Maggie.'

'Magsie!'

Tom pushed off: they were on the wide water—and he was face to face with Maggie. And then at last the full meaning of what had happened rushed upon his mind. It came with an overpowering force—a sudden realisation of the depths in life that had been outside his understanding—that understanding that he had imagined to be so keen and clear. The realisation was so powerful that he was unable to ask a question. They sat silently gazing at each other, Maggie with eyes of eager life looking out from a weary, beaten face—Tom pale with a new humbleness. Thought was busy, though the lips were silent; and, though Tom could ask no question, he guessed the story of the wonderful effort which her love had made possible.

At last a mist gathered over his blue-grey eyes, and the lips found a word that they could say—the old, childhood 'Magsie!'

Maggie could make no answer—only a long, deep sob of that mysterious, wonderful happiness which is so much like pain.

Tom rowed with untired strength and the boat was soon in the current of the river again. But a new danger was being carried towards them by the river. Some wooden beams and machinery had fallen from one of the store-houses on the river-front and huge pieces of it were being floated along. The sun was rising now and the grey flood was spread out in dreadful clearness around them. In dreadful clearness the hurrying, threatening masses floated onward.

A large company of men in a boat near the houses observed their danger and shouted: 'Get out of the current!'

But that could not be done at once; and Tom, looking round, saw death rushing on them. Huge objects, locked together by the racing water, made one wide mass across the stream.

'It's coming, Maggie!' Tom said in a deep voice, and took her in his arms...

The next instant the boat was no longer to be seen on the water—and the huge mass was hurrying on in dreadful triumph.

Soon the bottom of the boat reappeared.

The boat reappeared—but brother and sister had gone down locked together, never to be parted, living through again in one perfect moment the days when they had held each other's little hands in love, and wandered the flowery fields together.

Questions

Chapter

1 What was the miller's name?
2 Whose advice did Mrs Tulliver want?
Who was nine years old?
3 Why did Maggie interrupt the conversation?
Who was Mr Stelling?
4 What had happened to Tom's rabbits?
5 What was Tom's present for Maggie?
Why was Tom angry?
6 Who were Mrs Glegg, Mrs Pullet, and Mrs Deane?
7 Why was Mrs Pullet in tears?
Who was Lucy?
Who cut Maggie's hair at the back?
Who stood up for Maggie?
8 Who did Mr Tulliver quarrel with?
9 Who had lent Mr Tulliver £500?
Who was Mrs Moss?
10 Why did Tom have to learn Latin?
11 Where did Maggie see all the books?
What did Mr Stelling think about girls?
12 What was Pivart doing?
13 Who was the new pupil?
14 Who was Mr Poulter?
15 What happened to Tom's foot?
16 What was Tom's great fear?
17 What was Maggie's promise to Philip?
18 Who wanted Tom to go home?
19 Who had bought the rights to Mr Tulliver's property?
20 Where did Mrs Tulliver keep her 'treasures'?
21 Make a list of the people who were at the family council.
Who made Maggie angry?
Who had given Mr Tulliver a note for £300?
22 Where was Mr Deane's office?
Why could Maggie teach Tom accounts?
23 What was Mr Tulliver trying to find in his pocket?
What dates were already written in the Bible? (Write down those the book mentions, and guess others.)
What promise did Tom write in it?
24 Why did Mr Tulliver hate market days?

25 Describe the 'Red Deeps'.
What promise (Chapter 17) did Maggie not keep?
26 Who lent Tom some money?
Why had Philip never confessed his love?
What were Maggie's reasons for saying 'I hate you'?
27 How did Tom get the money?
28 Why did Mr Tulliver stop beating Wakem?
What was Mr Tulliver trying to say when he died?
29 Why had Maggie left the mill?
Why was Maggie alone in one of the boats?
30 Where was the boat when Maggie could see certain shapes?
Where was she trying to go?
Who was at the mill?
What caused the boat to overturn?

List of extra words

amends *good deeds done by a person to pay for harm that he has done*
channel *a ditch to lead water from one place to another*
clergyman *a priest (of the Church of England)*
cross *angry; often angry*
deformed *having something wrong with the shape of one's body (or a limb or limbs). The badly shaped part is a* deformity.
despise *feel scorn for*
disaster *a terrible accident*
disgrace *something that brings shame*
emotion *strong feeling*
go to law *ask (and pay for) the law courts to decide a case*
naughty *behaving badly*
passion *uncontrolled feelings*
queer *very unusual*
rascal *a person who cheats and is dishonest*
sob *draw breath in sharply when weeping; the sound of this*
timid *not brave*
triumph *(a sense of) victory;* triumphant = *enjoying victory*
vengeance *harming another to punish him for harm done to oneself*

Printed in Hong Kong by
Sheck Wah Tong Printing Press Ltd.